GLOBAL LINKS 2

English for International Business

Angela Blackwell

Longman

Global Links 2

Pearson Education, 10 Bank Street, White Plains, NY 10606

Vice president, director of publishing:	Allen Ascher
Senior acquisitions editor:	Marian Wassner
Senior development manager:	Penny Laporte
Senior development editor:	Carolyn Viola-John
Development editor:	Jennifer Bixby
Editorial assistant:	Nicole Santos Garrido
Vice president, director of design and production:	Rhea Banker
Executive managing editor:	Linda Moser
Production manager:	Alana Zdinak
Senior production editor:	Mike Kemper
Art director:	Patricia Wosczyk
Director of manufacturing:	Patrice Fraccio
Senior manufacturing buyer:	Dave Dickey
Photo research:	Photosearch, Inc.
Cover design:	Ann France
Book design and composition:	Word and Image Design

Illustrators: p.4, 10, 11, 16, 46, Gary Torrisi; p.35, 90, NSV Productions; p.32, 62, François Escalmel

Photo credits: From top to bottom, left to right. pp. 3, 8, 9, 14, 15, 21, 27, 33, 38, 39, 45, 51, 56, 57, 63, 68, 69, 70, 74, 75, 76, 80, and 81 by Gilbert Duclos; p.2, Courtesy of Plantronics, Inc. Plantronics and PLX are registered trademarks of Plantronics, Inc.; p.6(top), Walter Hodges/ CORBIS; p.6(bottom), Jose Luis Pelaez Inc./Corbis Stock Market; p.20, AP/Wide World Photos; p.22, Lwa-Dann Tardiff/Corbis Stock Market; p.26(top), Kelly-Mooney Photography/CORBIS; p.26(bottom), FPG International LLC; p.28, MTPA STOCK/Masterfile; p.30, Wernher Krutein and Bill Goidell/PHOTOVAULT.com; p.34, photos courtesy of United Parcel Services, Inc.; p.40, Bonnie Kamin/PhotoEdit; p.47, David Young-Wolff/PhotoEdit; p.50(a), Index Stock Imagery 2001; p.50(b), Michael Goldman/FPG International LLC; p.50(c), 2001 Fisher/Thatcher/Stone; p.52, Chris Ryan/Masterfile; p.53, 91, VCG/FPG International LLC; p.58, Rob Lewine/Corbis Stock Market; p.60, Pierre Tremblay/Masterfile; p.64(a), Carlos Domenech Photography/Leo de Wys; p.64(b), Index Stock Imagery/Lonnie Duka 2001; p.64(c), IFA Bilderteam/Leo de Wys; p.65(a), 92(a), CORBIS; p.65(b), 92(b), Christoph Wilhelm/FPG International LLC; p.67(top), William Whitehurst/Corbis Stock Market; p.67(bottom), Index Stock Imagery/Peter Ardito 2001; p.77, 2001 Tony Page/Stone; p.82, Ronnie Kaufman/Corbis Stock Market; p.83(top), Robert Holmes/CORBIS; p.83(middle), J. B. Grant/Leo de Wys; p.83 (bottom), Robert Holmes/CORBIS.

Side Banner photos: Unit 9 © Chris Ryan/Masterfile; All other units, Gilbert Duclos.

Cover photo: Computer-Generated Image of Globe/© Digital Art/CORBIS

ISBN: 0-13-088396-4

10–V082–10

Contents

Scope and Sequence

Unit	Social/Functional Language	Grammar	Business Culture	Writing	Numbers
1 Talking About Your Company	Asking and answering questions about companies *Plantronics designs and manufactures headsets.* *The company is marketing its products for home use.* *What does your company do?* *What is the company doing now?*	Simple present and present continuous (contrasted)	Business Dress Codes	A letter providing information about your company	Company performance (hundreds, thousands, and millions)
2 Making Conversation	Making small talk *You're in the computer industry, aren't you?* *That was an excellent meal, wasn't it?* *What part of Canada are you from?*	Tag questions	The Art of the Business Lunch	E-mail to a new client	Telephone numbers
3 Arranging Meetings and Schedules	Scheduling meetings and visits *I'm arriving on the 25th and leaving on the 27th.* *I'm out of the office on Monday.* *I've got meetings all day.* *Are you available the next day?*	Present tenses for the future Prepositions of time	Video-conferencing	Fax arranging a meeting	Airport Announcements; gate numbers
4 Getting Ahead	Describing work; discussing job qualifications *She's been CEO since July 1999.* *I'm with Marden Pharmaceuticals.* *What area are you in?* *How long have you been in this position?*	Present perfect with *for, since*	"Fast tracking" employees	Recommendation for a colleague	Survey results (percentages)
5 Turning a Company Around	Describing how a problem was solved; describing past performance *They introduced the Swatch brand in the early 1980's.* *It didn't sell very well, and we couldn't understand it.* *We had to lower the price.* *Sales went up immediately.*	Simple past *Could, had to*	Turnarounds	A business report	Sales figures (thousands)
6 Describing Processes	Describing a sequence of events; comparing processes *When the fruit is received at our plant, it is washed and sorted.* *How does your training system work?* *First, each employee is evaluated.* *Then, employees are ranked according to performance.*	Passive voice: simple present and past tenses	E-commerce	E-mail replies to customers	Business statistics (hundreds and millions)
7 Teamwork	Making requests, offers, and suggestions; negotiating and delegating tasks *Would you mind putting that in writing?* *Should I schedule a meeting?* *Let's get some lunch.* *Could you call Alan?*	Modals for requests, offers, and suggestions	Information Overload	A memo to managers	Survey results (single to three digit numbers)

Unit	Social/Functional Language	Grammar	Business Culture	Writing	Numbers
8 Managing Change	Describing changes at a company; past and present performance *We've restructured the company into three divisions.* *The company has appointed a new CEO.* *Sales have fallen this year.*	Present perfect (unspecified past)	Strategic Outsourcing	An annual report	Company performance (millions, percentages)
9 Clients and Customers	Responding to a complaint from a customer; negotiating a solution to a service problem *We have too many items in stock.* *We need more technical support.* *We don't have enough inventory.* *It's taking too long.*	Quantity Expressions: *too much, too many, not enough*	Total Quality Management	An apology to a customer	Invoice figures (dollar amounts)
10 Corporate Goals	Discussing business plans and expectations; preparing a business plan *We aim to develop cutting-edge technologies.* *We should maintain our strong financial position.* *We might consider joint ventures.* *We plan to introduce new services.*	Future forms: *plan to, aim to, expect to* *Might and should* for future	Preparing for Group Presentations	Department Goals: Report	Sales forecasts (hundred thousands)
11 Describing and Comparing products	Asking and answering questions about product features; comparing products *It's one of the fastest on the market.* *It's a better product.* *How does the Telec compare to the Portacall 100?* *Is it competitively priced?*	Comparative and superlative forms	Honesty in Selling	Memo to sales staff	Product specifications (measurements)
12 Challenges to Management	Describing project and staffing difficulties; discussing and comparing employee benefits *David has to have your sales figures by the end of the day.* *Can't you hire some more people?* *We won't be able to meet the deadline otherwise.*	Modals of obligation and possibility: *have to, need to, can, be able to* *Otherwise*	Leadership in the Twenty-first Century	Summary of a meeting	International survey results (thousands)
13 Motivation and Productivity	Giving an opinion about a course of action; discussing issues of motivation and productivity *If employees get performance bonuses, they'll be more productive.* *If we cut the budget, we won't be able to provide training.* *We'll be in real trouble if we don't do something.*	Real conditions with *if...will*	Making Meetings More Productive	An agenda for a meeting	Sales figures (dollars and yen)
14 Advertising Strategies	Discussing advertising strategies; proposing a website design *If we bought TV airtime, we'd be well over budget.* *What if we advertised on billboards?* *I don't think highway signs would be appropriate.* *It would be nice if we could do something dramatic.*	Unreal conditions with *if... could, would* Questions with *What if*	Marketing Across Cultures	Responding to a marketing survey	Internet users: predictions (millions and percentages)

Acknowledgments

The author and publisher wish to acknowledge with gratitude the following consultants, reviewers, and piloters who helped in the development of *Global Links*.

Consultants

Susan Caesar, Korea University, Seoul, Korea • **Ana Isabel Soares Delgado**, Instituto Brasil-Estados Unidos, Rio de Janeiro, Brazil • **Agustin Francisco**, Centro Cultural Dominico Americano, Santiago, Dominican Republic • **Mario Hernández-Lamia**, Universidad Iberoamericana Noroeste, Tijuana, Mexico • **María C. López-Adams**, University of Puerto Rico at Bayamón, Bayamón, Puerto Rico • **Marcela Martinez**, Universidad de los Andes, Santafé de Bogotá, Colombia • **Maria O'Conor**, GEOS Language System, Tokyo, Japan • **Julio Prin**, CVA La Trinidad, Caracas, Venezuela • **Grant Trew**, Nova Intercultural Institute, Tokyo, Japan.

Reviewers

Eugenio Aberto, Schola, Mexico City, Mexico • **Elton Carvalho**, Casa Thomas Jefferson, Brasília, Brazil • **Tom Edwards**, Aeon, Tokyo, Japan • **Meg Furlan**, The English Factory, São Paulo, Brazil • **Michael Glaser**, ALC Education Inc., Osaka, Japan • **Ioneti M. Javens**, The English Factory, São Paulo, Brazil • **Diana Jones**, Angloamericano, Mexico City, Mexico • **David Kendall**, Oe Dae Language Institute, Seoul, Korea • **Kevin Knight**, Kanda Gaigo Career College, Tokyo, Japan • **Karen Kuhel**, Associação, Brasil-América, Recife, Brazil • **Inés Román López**, Universidad de Tijuana, Tijuana, Mexico • **Márcia Sayuri Miasaki**. The English Factory, São Paulo, Brazil • **Megumi Okada**, OTC Inc., Osaka, Japan • **Brett Rockwood**, Nova Group, Toyko, Japan • **Isa Tirado Rodríguez**, Mexican Canadian Language Center, S.C., Zapopan, Jal, Mexico • **Jill Rachele Stucker**, Aeon, Tokyo, Japan • **Rosa E. Vásquez**, Centro Cultural Domínico Americano, Santo Domingo, Dominican Republic • **Orlando Vian Junior**, Seven English & Español, São Paulo, Brazil • **Marilia de Moura Zanella**, Associação Alumni, São Paulo, Brazil

Piloters

Tonya Balsdon, Interac Co., Ltd., Tokyo, Japan • **Sian Bollee**, Interac Co., Ltd., Tokyo, Japan • **Meg Furlan**, The English Factory, São Paulo, Brazil • **Jan Petter Isaksen**, Stratford Institute, León, Mexico • **Ioneti M. Javens**, The English Factory, São Paulo, Brazil • **Márcia Sayuri Miasaki**, The English Factory, São Paulo, Brazil • **Christina Wolff Vidal**, The English Factory, São Paulo, Brazil • **N. Walker**, Interac Co., Ltd., Hiroshima, Japan

The author would like to thank the following people for their assistance: Richard Pohl, Heloisa Amar, John Roedel, David Gonzalez Castro, Alfred Hoschek, and Alan Trottet.

I would also like to thank Allen Ascher, Marian Wassner, Penny Laporte, Jennifer Bixby, Carolyn Viola-John, and Michael Kemper at Pearson Education.

A.B.

Preface

Global Links: English for International Business is a three-level course that teaches the basic language and grammar structures needed to communicate in business. It is designed for adult students on the false beginner, low-intermediate, and intermediate levels who are employed as executives or are studying to enter the business world in that capacity. *Global Links* covers all four language skills, with special emphasis on the speaking and listening skills that managers need in international business.

FOCUS AND APPROACH

The goal of *Global Links* is to teach students the English they will need to communicate effectively in a professional environment. Students learn key vocabulary, social language, and structures through a progression of models and practice activities. Key language is recycled from module to module and unit to unit. Realistic tasks provide opportunities for students to produce the language they will need in common business situations.

Global Links is designed to meet the specialized needs of businesspeople and the instructors who teach them. Its modular design can flexibly accommodate students who are executives or managers and whose busy schedules may cause them to attend class irregularly. Although units are sequenced and reinforce previous learning, each can stand on its own. Within each unit, content is organized into self-contained two-page modules so that each lesson can be completed in a single class.

Global Links is written with small classes in mind. All speaking activities in *Global Links* center on pair work or tasks for small groups. The *Teacher's Manual* provides suggestions and alternative activities for teachers in one-to-one teaching situations and for teachers with larger classes who want to expand activities.

Features

- **Low-level language for high-level business people.** The clear, controlled pedagogical design of *Global Links* meets the language needs of lower-level students. At the same time, its sophisticated business content acknowledges the high level of real-world knowledge and experience that business-people bring to their study of English.

- **International focus.** *Global Links* exposes students to English as an international means of communication.

- **Authentic material about real companies.** *Global Links* offers authentic texts, documents, graphs, and charts with information about real companies and activities that have practical, real-world application.

- **Cultural information for doing business worldwide.** *Global Links* provides interesting, relevant information about doing business internationally and interacting with businesspeople from around the world.

- **Practice with numbers.** Many business situations involve numbers, which businesspeople need to set dates for meetings, discuss prices, and understand sales results. *Global Links* makes sure that businesspeople are comfortable using numbers in English by providing systematic practice with numbers as used in business contexts.

Course Length

Each level provides 40 to 45 hours of instruction, but the material may also be adapted to classes as short as 20 to 25 hours or as long as 50 to 60 hours of instruction. The course duration is flexible and is determined by the learning pace of the students, the attention and time given to writing in class, and the teacher's use of other materials.

ORGANIZATION OF STUDENT BOOKS 1 AND 2

The Student Book consists of fourteen units. Each has three, two-page modules: **Business Talk, Business Connections**, and **Global Communication**. Objectives for each module appear on the page to focus students' attention on their language learning target.

Module 1: Business Talk

Getting Started introduces the main social language, vocabulary, and grammatical focus of the unit. Students see or hear a language model, often in the context of authentic material, and then engage in a variety of controlled practice activities to "get started" using the language communicatively.

The *Conversation* presents the key social language and structures in a guided format. Substitution slots in the conversation add flexibility and ensure that students listen to their partner.

Each conversation is followed by *Pronunciation Focus*. This section uses sentences drawn or adapted from the *Conversation* to highlight different features of spoken English and emphasize the development of better rhythm, intonation, and stress.

Module 2: Business Connections

The *Listening* page builds students' aural comprehension abilities through a variety of listening texts and activities that train the students in two important listening skills: listening for general meaning and context and listening for specific information. The recordings are spoken at natural speed and include a variety of native and nonnative English speakers' accents, exposing students to the different kinds of spoken English they will encounter in business situations.

An information gap, pair work, role-play, or small group activity on the *Speaking* page moves students along from controlled practice to using the language they have learned in the unit more freely. The speaking activities reinforce the structures and vocabulary presented in earlier parts of the unit. Additionally, these activities develop students' ability to exchange information and ideas in ways that are meaningful to their work environment and personal career.

Module 3: Global Communication

The *Reading* section features informative excerpts from business publications, magazines, and newspapers about business practices and customs in different cultures. Each passage is followed by a task that focuses on a skill that all businesspeople need: reading for specific information.

The reading passage and task serve as a springboard for *Talk About It*. The questions prompt simple classroom discussion on the theme and issues of the reading. In Book 2, cross-cultural questions are marked with the symbol of a globe.

The *Writing* section provides information about the form and content of basic business writing with particular emphasis on e-mail correspondence. First students see models of various types of business writing. They then follow directions to compose their own e-mail, fax, letter, report, etc.

Each unit of Book 1 concludes with two *number* exercises. Most students are familiar with the basic numbers in English, but they may have difficulty using them with ease in business situations. The listening and speaking exercises in this section improve students' ability to use numbers in a business context. In Book 2, the *numbers* activities are contextualized and may appear with a listening or in another module.

The book concludes with the *Activity File* for pair work, the *Summary Language*, which presents key vocabulary, expressions, and grammar for each unit, and a *Glossary* of important business terms contained in the text. Book 2 also includes *Extra Speaking Activities* which provide more open-ended communication practice.

COMPONENTS OF THE COURSE

Complete Audio Program

The Complete Audio Program CDs and Cassettes provide recordings for the *Getting Started, Conversation, Pronunciation Focus, Listening,* and *Numbers* sections of the Student Book.

Student CD

The Student CD, which is included in the Student Book, provides recordings of the *Conversation* sections (with the exception of the alternate phrases), the *Pronunciation Focus* sections, and in Book 2, the *Numbers* section. In Book 1, one of the exercises in the *Numbers* section is provided.

Phrase Book

The Phrase Book, which is also included in the Student Book, provides a portable, easy-to-use reference guide to the key language and structures needed in most business situations and a glossary of business terms.

Teacher's Manual

The *Teacher's Manual* supports teachers by giving both general and page-by-page teaching suggestions, including a teacher's script of short, easy-to-understand instructions that may be used in class; a tapescript of all recordings on the Audio CD; answer keys to the activities in the Student Book; and expansion activities and photocopiables for each unit.

Tests

Each level of **Global Links** includes a Test Package that provides unit-by-unit assessment quizzes and two longer exams, one designed to assess students at mid-course, the other at the end of the course. All tests include TOEIC-type questions, which familiarize students with the format of this widely used test in the business world.

A set of Placement Tests will assist in placing students at the most appropriate level of the **Global Links** program.

Companion Website

The Global Links companion website (http://www.longman.com/globallinks) provides numerous resources for teachers and students, including vocabulary exercises; TOEIC-type audio tests; pair practice for building conversation skills; and TOEIC-type reading comprehension exercises. Most exercises are self-grading.

There are also community features, links to other sites for business reading practice, and links to sample TOEIC tests. The site is periodically updated and expanded with new resources.

GLOBAL LINKS

2

Talking About Your Company

BUSINESS TALK

GETTING STARTED

1. Read and listen to the article about Plantronics.

Plantronics, Inc., designs and manufactures lightweight headsets for telephones, mobile phones, and personal computers. The company sells its products worldwide and has offices in 19 countries. The head office is in Santa Cruz, California. Plantronics employs more than 2,000 people.

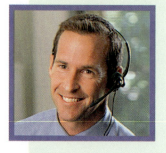

Plantronics is currently marketing its products for home use. More and more people now are using headsets to listen to music or play video games on their computers. As a result, Plantronics is developing a new generation of headsets for the personal computer and mobile telephone.

Source: Plantronics

2. Listen. Circle the correct choice.

    a. Plantronics *designs/is designing* lightweight headsets.

    b. The company *has/is having* offices in 19 countries.

    c. Plantronics *employs/is employing* more than 2,000 people.

    d. The market for headsets *grows/is growing* fast.

    e. Currently, Plantronics *develops/is developing* headsets for personal use.

3. Work with a partner. Talk about your company. Use the words in the box.

> We manufacture . . .   We sell . . .
> We supply . . .   We design . . .
> We provide services for . . .
>
> At the moment, . . .   we're hiring . . .
> Right now, . . .   we're developing . . .
> Currently, . . .   we're opening . . .
>   we're expanding . . .

Go to page 98 for Summary Language

CONVERSATION

What does your company do?

🎧 **4.** Read and listen to the conversation.

What does your company do?

We're a financial services company.

· We provide financial services.

Oh. Are you based in the United States?

Our head office is in Atlanta, but we have offices all over Latin America.

· Where's your head office?

· worldwide

So, what are you doing here?

Right now, we're working with a bank in Rio.

· in Brazil · opening an office

That's interesting.

And we're opening an office in São Paulo, too.

· Really?

🎧 Listen again and repeat.

5. Practice the conversation with a partner.

Pronunciation Focus: *Wh–* questions

🎧 **6.** Listen and repeat.

a. What does your company do?
b. So, what are you doing here?
c. Where's your head office?

LISTENING

We're growing pretty fast right now.

🎧 **1.** Listen to this presentation at a job fair in Mexico City. Look at the pictures. Which presentation did you hear? Check (✓) a or b.

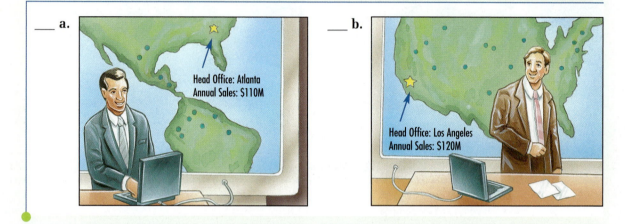

___ a.

Head Office: Atlanta
Annual Sales: $110M

___ b.

Head Office: Los Angeles
Annual Sales: $120M

🎧 **2.** Listen again and complete the notes about the presentation.

> ### Business Solutions
> (a) **Business software** and consulting services. Head office in
> (b) _____ ; offices all over the world.
> (c) _____ employees (most in US & Europe)
> 2,500 Clients (large corporations; small and medium-sized businesses)
> Annual income: (d) $_____ million
> In Mexico since (e) _____ ; number of accounts (f) _____
> Also in Brazil, Venezuela, and (g) _____

NUMBERS

🎧 **3.** Listen to the information about the company's clients and net income. Complete the chart.

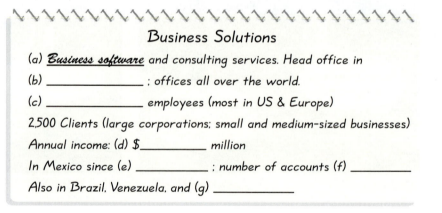

Year	Number of Clients	Net Income
1996	500	$ _____ million
1998	_____	_____
2000	_____	_____
This year	_____	_____

🎧 Listen again and check your answers.

SPEAKING

What type of company is NTT?

4. Speaker A, use this page. Speaker B, see the Activity File on page 86.

Speaker A, ask Speaker B for the information you need and complete the chart. Use the questions in the box below.

Conversation Strategies

Clarifying information
- Could you repeat that?
- Excuse me?
- How do you spell that?

> What type of company is _____?   Where is the head office of _____?
>
> How many employees does it have?   What is the company doing now?

Example

Speaker A: What type of company is NTT Communications?
Speaker B: It's a telecommunications company.

NTT Communications
Type of company: *Telecommunications*
Head office: Tokyo, Japan
Employees: _____
Current activities: Expanding its global internet services

Hanjin Shipping
Type of company: Shipping and transportation
Head office: _____
Employees: 3,400
Current activities: _____

Unibanco
Type of company: _____
Head office: São Paulo, Brazil
Employees: _____
Current activities: Developing business–to–business Internet services in Latin America

5. Now answer Speaker B's questions.

6. What do you know about these companies? Talk about the ones that you know. Use the phrases in the box.

> It sells/manufactures/provides . . .
> It's based in . . .
> Right now, it's . . .

Go to the extra speaking activity on page 93.

READING

Business Dress Codes

1. Read the article.

Business Culture

Dress codes are rapidly changing in the world of business. In companies across the United States, the business suit and tie are disappearing from the workplace, and casual office wear—slacks and a sports jacket for men, pants or a skirt and a jacket for women—is becoming more and more popular. "Dress down Friday" (a day when employees are permitted to wear casual clothes) is spreading to the other weekdays, and this trend will probably continue.

 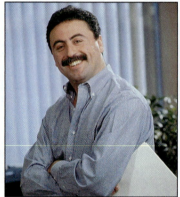

In a poll of 3,700 executives by Management Recruiters International of Cleveland, Ohio, 40 percent believed that the business suit is becoming a thing of the past. Many executives believe that business people will not wear suits at all ten years from now, not even to job interviews.

Source: Management Review

2. Write *T* (true) or *F* (false) according to the article.

a. This article is about what to wear for an interview. __

b. Business people dress informally more often now. __

c. Nowadays, people wear business suits on "dress down Fridays." __

d. Many of the executives in the poll think that business people will dress more casually in the future. __

Talk About It

3. Discuss these questions.

a. What do men and women wear to work in your company?

b. Is the business suit disappearing in your workplace?

c. Is it important to dress formally in your industry? Why or why not?

WRITING

A Letter Providing Information About Your Company

4. Read the letter.

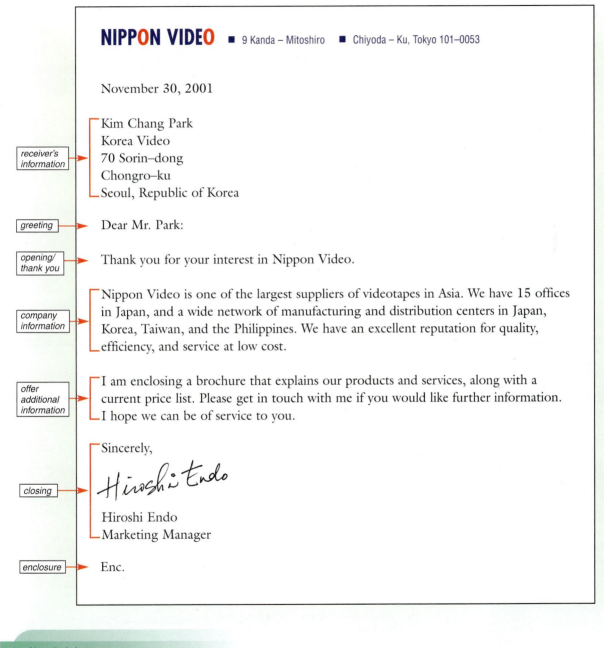

NIPPON VIDEO ■ 9 Kanda – Mitoshiro ■ Chiyoda – Ku, Tokyo 101–0053

November 30, 2001

receiver's information →
Kim Chang Park
Korea Video
70 Sorin–dong
Chongro–ku
Seoul, Republic of Korea

greeting → Dear Mr. Park:

opening/ thank you → Thank you for your interest in Nippon Video.

company information →
Nippon Video is one of the largest suppliers of videotapes in Asia. We have 15 offices in Japan, and a wide network of manufacturing and distribution centers in Japan, Korea, Taiwan, and the Philippines. We have an excellent reputation for quality, efficiency, and service at low cost.

offer additional information →
I am enclosing a brochure that explains our products and services, along with a current price list. Please get in touch with me if you would like further information. I hope we can be of service to you.

Sincerely,

Hiroshi Endo

closing →
Hiroshi Endo
Marketing Manager

enclosure → Enc.

Useful Language

■ We are recognized as a world leader in _____.
■ Enclosed is a catalogue that describes _____.
■ Please feel free to call me for further information.

Write a letter responding to a request for information about your company's services or products. Describe your company, its size and location(s), and its main activities. If you prefer, use one of the companies on page 5.

Making Conversation

OBJECTIVES

- To make small talk

- To initiate and continue a conversation

- To write a follow-up message after an initial meeting

GETTING STARTED

1. Read the questions. Then match the questions with the answers.

_3_ **a.** You like Thai food, don't you?

___ **b.** Bangkok is an exciting city, isn't it?

___ **c.** You're in the computer industry, aren't you?

___ **d.** You like sports, don't you?

1. Yes, I'm a software engineer.

2. Yes, there's so much to see and do.

3. I'm not sure. What's it like?

4. Oh yes, I'm a big soccer fan. How about you?

🎧 Listen and check your answers.

🎧 **2.** Listen and complete the conversations.

a. A: This is your first visit to New York, ___isn't it___?
B: Yes, it is.

b. A: It's a wonderful city, _____?
B: Oh, yes. There's so much to see and do.

c. A: You're in the computer industry, _____?
B: Yes. What about you?

d. A: That was an excellent meal, _____?
B: Delicious. I love Mexican food.

e. A: You live in Buenos Aires, _____?
B: Yes. Have you been to Argentina?

f. A: You don't follow soccer much in the US, _____?
B: No, but it's getting more popular now.

🎧 Listen again and check your answers.

3. Practice the conversations above with a partner. Take turns asking and answering the questions.

Go to page 99 for Summary Language

CONVERSATION

You're from the United States, aren't you?

🎧 **4.** Read and listen to the conversation.

What would you like to drink? Coffee? Tea? Mineral water?

I'll have some mineral water, thanks.

• Can I get you something
• I'd like

You're from the United States, aren't you?

No. Actually, I'm from Canada.

• Are you American?
• I'm Canadian

What part of Canada are you from?

Calgary.

• Where do you live in Canada?

Oh, really? That's in the mountains, isn't it?

That's right. We do a lot of skiing there.

• Calgary?
• Right.

🎧 Listen again and repeat.

5. Practice the conversation with a partner.

Pronunciation Focus: Tag questions

🎧 **6.** Listen and repeat.

    a. You're from the United States, aren't you?

    b. That's in the mountains, isn't it?

    c. This is your first visit, isn't it?

BUSINESS CONNECTIONS

LISTENING

Are you going to São Paulo on business?

🎧 **1.** Listen to the conversations. Look at the pictures. Who is speaking? Number the pictures 1–4.

___ a.

___ b.

1 c.

___ d.

2. Match the questions with the responses.

___ **a.** How's it going?

___ **b.** Would you like some help with the menu?

___ **c.** Are you going to São Paulo on business?

___ **d.** Welcome to Mexico. Did you have a good trip?

___ **e.** Could I get you a cup of coffee?

1. No thanks. I just had some.

2. Fine. We're very busy.

3. It was very nice, thank you.

4. Oh yes, please. What do you recommend?

5. Yes. We have a contract with a telephone company there.

🎧 **Listen and check your answers.**

SPEAKING

Do you live in California?

3. Work with a partner. Read the situations below and have conversations with your partner. Continue the conversations as long as possible.

1. On a plane to Los Angeles

Speaker A, you are going to the US for a one-week training program in Los Angeles, California. Start a conversation with Speaker B. Talk about travel and work.

Speaker B, you are returning to the US after a vacation. You live and work in Los Angeles. Talk about travel and work.

> #### Example
>
> A: Do you live in California?
> B: Yes, I'm from Los Angeles.

2. In a Restaurant

Speaker B, you are meeting a business associate who is visiting from another country. Ask about his or her trip and then talk about things to do, such as sightseeing, sports, musical events, and theater.

Speaker A, you are on a visit from another country. Talk about what you want to see and do.

> #### Example
>
> B: Is this your first visit to _____?
> A: Yes, it's a wonderful city.

Conversation Strategies

Making Small Talk
- You're from ___, aren't you?
- Is this your first visit to ___?
- Do you like ___?
- You enjoy ___, don't you?
- Tell me, do you follow ___? (a sport)
- What about you?

Go to the extra speaking activity on page 93.

READING

The Art of the Business Lunch

1. Read the article.

Business Culture

The business lunch is an excellent way to improve a relationship with a client. However, since eating is a very social thing, it's easy to get distracted. So plan what you would like to discuss, just like a business meeting.

It helps to think of the business lunch as having a specific beginning, middle, and end. Begin with a minute or two of small talk, and then talk about business until the food arrives. During the meal, put away the paperwork and focus on getting to know your client. Avoid food that is messy or difficult to eat.

The person who does the inviting should pay for the meal. If you think your clients will insist on paying, pay the bill in advance. Arrive earlier than your guests. Do not order anything while you are waiting for them. When the guests arrive, stand up and shake hands. If they are late, wait about 15 minutes before you telephone their office.

The three–hour power lunch has largely disappeared in North America. Nowadays, the appropriate length for the business lunch is about 1 1/2 hours: a shorter, more productive meeting that still leaves time for work afterwards.

Source: The Toronto Star

2. Check (✓) what you should and should not do at a business lunch according to the article.

	Yes	No
a. Plan what you would like to discuss before a business lunch.	✓	___
b. Make small talk for a long time before discussing business.	___	___
c. Order a meal that isn't difficult to eat.	___	___
d. It's OK to be late if you are inviting.	___	___
e. It's OK to order a drink while you wait for your guest.	___	___
f. If your guests are late, you should leave the restaurant after 15 minutes.	___	___

Talk About It

3. Discuss the questions.

a. Do you agree with the advice in the article?

b. What advice would you give a visiting colleague about business meals in your country?

WRITING

E-mail to a New Client

4. Read the e–mail.

Alex Kim

From: akim@allgolf.com
Sent: September 11, 3:23pm
To: rdario@gla.com.mx
Subject: **Executec lunch**

Mr. Dario:

It was a pleasure meeting you at the Executec lunch last week. I enjoyed our discussion, and I appreciated your comments about our products.

As promised, I am sending you some information on our Deluxe range of golf bags. These are made of a new synthetic fiber that is both strong and lightweight.

Please feel free to contact me if you have any questions or if you would like to see samples of our products.

Alex Kim
Sales Manager

Useful Language

■ I appreciated your feedback about _____.

■ As I mentioned during lunch, _____.

Write an e-mail to someone you recently met who is interested in your company's products or services. In your message:

• say how much you enjoyed meeting him/her
• follow up on any promises or requests made
• say how that person can contact you in the future

NUMBERS

🎧 **5.** Listen. Correct the mistakes in the messages. Then listen again.

a.
MESSAGE

From: *Bob Green*
                1
(303) 993-9802
bgreen@stpaul.edu

wants info about
training courses

b.
MESSAGE

From: *Paulo Ferreira*

(55-1) 819-7790
(Brazil)
paulo@ombanco.com.br
call about visit next
week

c.
MESSAGE

From: *Helena Schwartz*

(507) 623-1768
hs3@wonderlink.com

e-mail application form

d.
MESSAGE

From: *Masato Gomo*

(81-45) 910-0442
(Japan)

please call him

Check your answers with a partner. Say the numbers.

Arranging Meetings and Schedules

BUSINESS TALK

GETTING STARTED

🎧 **1.** Anita Mendez is calling Paul Chan to schedule a meeting. Look at Paul's schedule. Then listen and write the time of the meeting on the calendar.

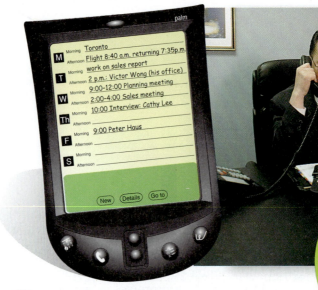

palm

M	Morning	Toronto
	Afternoon	Flight 8:40 a.m. returning 7:35 p.m.
T	Morning	work on sales report
	Afternoon	2 p.m.: Victor Wong (his office)
W	Morning	9:00-12:00 Planning meeting
	Afternoon	2:00-4:00 Sales meeting
Th	Morning	10:00 Interview: Cathy Lee
	Afternoon	
F	Morning	9:00 Peter Haus
	Afternoon	
S	Morning	
	Afternoon	

(New) (Details) (Go to)

🎧 **2.** Listen again. Fill in the missing words.

What does Paul say about . . .

a. Monday?

_____*I'm out of the office*_____ on Monday.

b. Tuesday?

_____ in the afternoon.

c. Wednesday?

_____ all day.

d. Thursday?

_____ in the morning.

3. Work with a partner. Talk about your schedule next week. Use the words in the box.

Example

A: *I'm going to New York on Monday.*
B: *I've got a sales presentation in Tokyo on Monday afternoon.*

> in the morning
> on _____ afternoon
> all day
> on _____ (day of the week)

Go to page 100 for Summary Language

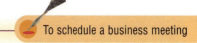
CONVERSATION

Could we set up a meeting?

🎧 **4.** Read and listen to the conversation.

I'm coming to Sydney next month. Could we set up a meeting?

Yes, of course. When can you come to the office?

Well, I'm arriving on the 25th and leaving on the 27th.

How about the 25th? I'm free after two.

- Can we arrange   • make it   • I'm available

Hmm. I'm afraid I can't make it then. I've got meetings all day.

OK. Are you available the next day? Around eleven o'clock?

Well, twelve would be better if it's OK with you.

That sounds good. I'll see you on the 26th at twelve o'clock.

- I'm sorry, but I'm busy on the 25th.   • How about   • convenient for you   • That's OK with me.

🎧 Listen again and repeat.

5. Practice the conversation with a partner.

Pronunciation Focus: Stress

🎧 **6.** Listen and repeat.

    a. I'm arriving on the twenty-fifth.

    b. I'm available after two.

    c. I'm afraid I can't make it.

    d. I've got meetings all day.

LISTENING

It's a pretty full schedule.

1. Margaret Grant and Joe Verducci are traveling to Mexico to visit a manufacturing plant. They are discussing their schedule. Listen. Write *T* (true) or *F* (false).

a. When they arrive, Margaret and Joe are going to the head office. ____

b. There is a design presentation on Monday before lunch. ____

c. They will have time for sightseeing on Tuesday. ____

2. Listen again and complete the schedule.

MONDAY		TUESDAY	
(a) _9:30_	Flight arrives in Mexico City		
	Meet José Ferraro at airport	10:00	Meet with production (f) _____
	Go to (b) _____		and engineers
11:00	Meet (c) _____	12:00	General (g) _____
12:30	(d) _____	2:00	Lunch
	at head office		
(e) _____	Lunch	(h) _____	Go to airport
4:00	Meet Director of Latin American operations		

NUMBERS

3. Listen to the airport announcements. Write the gate number and circle the correct comments.

DEPARTURES						
TIME	FLIGHT	DESTINATION	GATE	COMMENTS		
08:45	WA 194	Singapore	86	(now boarding)	delayed	(go to gate)
08:50	AA 103	London		now boarding	delayed	go to gate
09:20	NA 560	Taipei		now boarding	delayed	go to gate
08:45	WA 191	Mexico City		now boarding	delayed	go to gate
09:00	AA 182	Frankfurt		now boarding	delayed	go to gate

Listen again and check your answers.

SPEAKING

When are you available?

4. Speaker A, use this page. Speaker B, see the Activity File on page 87.

Speaker A, you will be in Speaker B's city on business next week. Look at your schedule below and arrange a time to meet. Use the phrases in the box. Write the appointment in your schedule.

> I'm available after . . .
> I'm afraid I can't make it . . .
> I'm sorry, I'm busy . . .
> So, when can you make it?
> How about . . . ?

Example

A: *I'm coming to (your city) next week for a few days. Could we set up a meeting?*
B: *Of course. When are you available?*

MONDAY		
June 13th	Morning:	9:30 flight arrives: go to Plaza Hotel
	Afternoon:	
	Evening:	Dinner, Margaret Ono
TUESDAY		
June 14th	Morning:	10:00 meeting: Ron Mendez (a lunch?)
	Afternoon:	Trade show: presentation 2:00 p.m.
	Evening:	
WEDNESDAY		
June 15th	Morning:	Trade show: presentations 9-1
	Afternoon:	
	Evening:	
THURSDAY		
June 16th	Morning:	8:30 flight departs: leave hotel at 7:15 a.m.

5. Look at your own schedule for next week. Make arrangements with Speaker B for the following:
- a meeting in the morning
- a visit to a company in the afternoon
- dinner one evening

Conversation Strategies

Accepting an Invitation
- I'd like to (have dinner).
- That would be very nice. Thank you.
- That would be great.

Go to the extra speaking activity on page 93.

READING

It's Time to Try Videoconferencing

1. Read the article.

Business Culture

Thanks to videoconferencing, attorneys Fred Parnon and George Pratt have become "virtual" partners in Parnon's office. Two years ago, Parnon set up a videoconferencing system between his New York City office and Pratt's suburban home, so that Pratt could avoid the long commute into the city. The partners keep the system on all the time. "It's as if we're in the same office with our desks touching," says Parnon. "I miss him when it's turned off." The technology "lets us see each other's face and hand gestures, which gives us much better communication than we would have just talking on the phone," says Parnon.

More and more small business CEOs are using this increasingly affordable and available business tool. Apart from reducing travel, videoconferencing systems have other useful features. For example, using a function called a shared whiteboard, participants at great distances can work on the same document at the same time, or see the results instantly on their computer screens.

While videoconferencing is not yet as quick and easy as a telephone call, analysts say the day is coming. So along with your cell phone and beeper numbers, e-mail address, and fax number, you might also need to put your videoconferencing station number on your business card.

Source: Your Company (© Time Inc.)

2. Match the beginnings and endings of the sentences according to the article.

_3_ **a.** Parnon and Pratt set up a videoconferencing system

___ **b.** Parnon prefers video-conferencing to the telephone

___ **c.** Small business CEOs like videoconferencing

___ **d.** Videoconferencing systems are also useful

___ **e.** Executives may soon list station numbers on their business cards

1. because people in different locations can work on material at the same time.

2. because the use of video-conferencing will be increasing.

3. because Pratt wanted to work from his home.

4. because he can see his partner's face and hand gestures.

5. because it reduces the amount of business travel they have to do.

Talk About It

3. Discuss these questions.

a. How is videoconferencing useful, or how could it be useful, in your work?

b. In what situations would you prefer to have a personal meeting?

c. Is videoconferencing useful when there are language or cultural differences? Why or why not?

WRITING

A Fac
A Fax

4. Anita Mendez is requesting a meeting. Read her fax.

ACC, Inc.

Fax: 312-664-2602
Phone: 312-663-1457

Fax

To: Dong-Jin Kang   **From:** Anita Mendez
Fax: (82-2) 744-0279   **Pages:** 1
Company: KBC Korea   **Date:** October 4, 2001
RE: Visit to Seoul

Message

Dear Mr. Kang:

It was a pleasure to meet you again at the trade show last week.

I am visiting Seoul next month, and I would like to show you our newest accounting software program for small businesses.

I will be in Seoul from the 12th until the 15th of November. If possible, I would like to schedule an appointment for the 13th or 14th. Could you please suggest a day and time that would be convenient for you?

I look forward to hearing from you.

Write a fax to Anita Mendez. Say that you will be out of town on the 13th and 14th. Suggest another day and time.

Useful Language

- If possible, I would like to _____.
- Could you please suggest _____?
- I'm afraid I won't be available _____.

Getting Ahead

Go to page 101 for Summary Language

OBJECTIVES

■ To ask and answer questions about work

■ To describe and discuss job qualifications

■ To write a recommendation for a colleague

BUSINESS TALK

GETTING STARTED

1. Read and listen to the information about Carly Fiorina.

Carleton (Carly) Fiorina is the president, chief executive officer, and chairwoman of Hewlett–Packard Company. Hewlett–Packard is a leading global provider of computer products and services. Fiorina has been at Hewlett–Packard since 1997. She has been CEO since July 1999, making her the first female CEO of one of America's 20 largest corporations.

Fiorina has held top management positions for nearly 20 years. Before 1997, she worked at AT&T and Lucent Technologies. At Lucent, she was president of its largest division, the Global Sevices Provider Business.

In 1999, Fortune magazine named her "the most powerful woman in American business."

2. Answer the questions.

a. Who is Carly Fiorina?
b. How long has she been with Hewlett–Packard?
c. How long has she been in her current position?
d. How long has she worked in management?
e. Where did she work before Hewlett–Packard?
f. What did she do at Lucent Technologies?

3. Choose two possible answers from sentences 1–6 for each question below.

1. I'm an accountant.
2. For about ten years.
3. At Norcom. I was a sales director.
4. Since 1998.
5. I'm in telecommunications.
6. I was in the computer industry.

a. What do you do?	_1_	___
b. How long have you been in this position?	___	___
c. Where did you work before this?	___	___

4. Now take turns asking and answering the questions above with a partner.

CONVERSATION

What area are you in?

🎧 **4.** Read and listen to the conversation.

· admire your work
· that's good to hear

· do you work in   · Research and development   · Have you been with Marden a long time?   · Since I got my degree.

🎧 Listen again and repeat.

5. Practice the conversation with a partner.

Pronunciation **F**ocus: Showing interest

🎧 **6.** Listen and repeat.

    a. I really enjoyed the presentation.
    b. I really admire your work.
    c. I'm delighted to hear that.
    d. That's good to hear.

LISTENING

Have you always worked in banking?

🎧 **1.** Bob Coronado is vice president of marketing at an international investment bank in New York. Look at Bob's employment history. Listen and number the items 1–4 (4 = his most recent position).

_____ **a.** Director, International Marketing
PS Software, Inc., Sunnytown, California

__4__ **b.** Vice President of Marketing
Northwest Bank, New York, New York

_____ **c.** Worked in the sales department
MEG Systems, Hanover, Germany

_____ **d.** Director of Marketing
Northwest Bank, New York, New York

🎧 **2.** Listen again and complete the sentences.

a. Before he went into banking, Bob worked in the
_____computer_____ industry.

b. After he graduated, Bob worked at _____.

c. He went back to school to study _____.

d. He worked in the computer industry for _____.

e. He stopped working in the computer industry because

_____.

f. He went to China for _____.

g. Bob has been Vice President since _____.

h. He has been with Northwest Bank for _____.

SPEAKING

How long has he had this job?

3. Speaker A use this page. Speaker B, see the Activity File on page 88.

   You and Speaker B are colleagues at Northwest Bank. You want to hire an executive assistant and are considering two candidates.

   Speaker A, read about Cristina Lee. Answer Speaker B's questions.

   #### Example

   B: What is Christina doing now?
   A: She's an executive assistant at the Santa Clara branch.

Name:	Cristina Lee
Current position:	Executive Assistant, Northwest Bank, Santa Clara branch
How long in this position:	8 years
Previous experience:	Administrative Assistant, Northwest Bank, Santa Clara branch (5 years) Bank teller, National Bank (3 years)
Computer skills:	Needs training
Education:	BA degree
Other information:	Cristina's boss recommends her highly, but some coworkers find her hard to work with.

4. Ask Speaker B about Paul Martin. Use the questions in the box as well as your own. Complete the chart.

What's he doing now?	Where did he . . . ?
How long has he had this job?	Does he have good . . . ?

Name:	Paul Martin
Current position:	
How long in this position:	
Previous experience:	
Computer skills:	
Education:	
Other information:	Paul's father is a good friend of the bank president. Paul will work very hard.

Conversation Strategies

Disagreeing Politely
- I'm not sure I agree.
- Do you think so?
- Yes, but don't you think _____?

Go to the extra speaking activity on page 94.

5. Talk about the candidates. Look at all the information. Who do you want to hire? Give two reasons.

READING

"Fast-Tracking" Employees: A Smart Move

1. Read the article.

Business Culture

The appointment of Carly Fiorina as president and CEO of Hewlett–Packard is an example of two major trends in corporate America. First, female executives are gradually rising to the top. Second, companies tend to hire top managers from outside rather than promote from within the company.

Very few American companies train employees well enough to become leaders of the company, says William C. Byham, author of the book *Grow Your Own Leaders*. Some companies do have a list of possible employees for top jobs, but they fear that these people do not have the skills or training to take over if a key person leaves. Others have great hopes for some employees, but don't tell them.

Byham says that upper management must be strongly committed to developing its own leaders. That in itself can be a problem because some managers don't want to train people to take their place.

According to Byham, it is important to identify several people for the "fast track," and give them assignments that will develop their management skills. And finally, it is important to make sure that people who are on the "fast track" know that they have a place in the organization's future.

Source: San Francisco Examiner

2. Write *T* (true) or *F* (false) according to the article.

a. Most American CEOs are promoted from within the company. _____F_____

b. Most American companies plan for the future leadership of the company. _____

c. Many American companies do not believe that their employees can fill top management positions. _____

d. Some managers do not want to prepare a person to take over their job. _____

e. It is important for companies to identify leaders inside the company. _____

f. It is important to tell employees that they have a future in the company. _____

Talk About It

3. Discuss the following questions.

a. Do you think it's important for a company to train managers for top positions? Or, is it better to hire leaders from outside the company?

b. Why is it important to let employees know that they are on the "fast track?"

WRITING

A Recommendation

4. Read the memo.

MEMO

To: Craig Warner
From: Tony Matsumoto
RE: Martin Chang
Date: November 11, 2001

As you know, we are closing our Atlanta office, and I'd like to recommend Martin Chang for the position that is open in your territory, Midwestern Regional Sales Manager.

Martin has been with the company for seven years. He worked in the Northeast area for two years. He then moved to Altanta and joined our sales team.

For the past two years, Martin has been our top sales rep. Last year, he generated an impressive $750,000 in sales.

Martin builds good relationships with clients and has strong leadership skills and technical knowledge. He works well in a team and is loyal to the company. I believe he is an excellent candidate for promotion to the regional sales manager position.

Will you be at the St. Louis meeting next week? I'll be there and will be happy to discuss Martin's application with you.

Tony

Tony Matsumoto

Useful Language

- He/She has been with the company for ____ years.
- He/She first worked in ____.
- He/She took over as ____.
- For the past ____ years, he/she has worked in ____.

Write a memo. Recommend someone you know for a promotion. Give reasons for your recomendation.

NUMBERS

5. Listen. Fill in the percentages.

Number of executives in survey:	4,500
a. changed positions	71%
b. held three or more positions	___
c. worked for two or more companies	___
d. moved to another area	___
e. lost their jobs	___
f. started their own businesses	___

Source: Management Review

Check your answers with a partner. Say the numbers.

Turning a Company Around

BUSINESS TALK

GETTING STARTED

1. Read and listen to the article.

Between the mid–70s and 1983, the Swiss share of the global watch industry fell to just 9 percent. Foreign competitors dominated the market. Then Swiss watch manufacturers decided to work together and sell under one brand name. They introduced the Swatch brand in the early 1980s and saved the industry. Sales rose steadily, and by 1993, the Swiss share of the global watch industry was up to 55 percent.

In the late 1950s, a Honda sales team went to America to introduce the company's big motorcycles. The US market for large motorcycles was already dominated by an American company. But there was hope for the smaller bikes. So the team changed direction and sold small bikes instead. The strategy was a success.

Source: Management Review

2. Work with a partner. Ask and answer the questions.

a. How did Swiss watch makers increase their market share?
b. What happened after they introduced the Swatch brand?
c. What did Honda want to sell in the US at first?
d. Why did Honda change its strategy?

3. Work with a partner. Discuss your company or a company you know. Talk about problems it had. How did it solve the problems? Use the words in the box or your own ideas.

Example

Last year my company faced increasing competition.

Last year A few years ago In the early 90s In the late 90s	(company)	couldn't sell its new product. had falling sales. faced increasing competition. lost market share.

OBJECTIVES

▪ To describe how a problem was solved

▪ To describe past performance

▪ To write a report describing action taken

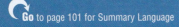
Go to page 101 for Summary Language

CONVERSATION

We couldn't understand it.

🎧 **4.** Read and listen to the conversation.

The X–200 laptop is selling well now. Wasn't there a problem with that model?

Yes, there was. It didn't sell **very** well, and we couldn't understand it.

• perform

Really? **Did you figure it out?**

Yes. We found that customers didn't like the keyboard, and the price was too high.

• Did you find out why?

Well, we redesigned the keyboard, and we had to **lower** the price.

So what did you do?

• reduce

Yes. Our sales **went up immediately.**

Did your strategy work?

• Did that solve the problem?   • increased right away

🎧 Listen again and repeat.

5. Practice the conversation with a partner.

Pronunciation Focus: *Couldn't/Didn't*

🎧 **6.** Listen and repeat.

    a. It didn't sell very well.

    b. We couldn't understand it.

    c. We couldn't figure it out.

    d. The customers didn't like the keyboard.

BUSINESS CONNECTIONS

LISTENING

It was a very exciting time.

1. An automobile sales manager is describing the sales performance of the Coupe XL.

Listen. Which graph is the sales manager referring to? Check (✓) *a*, *b*, or *c*.

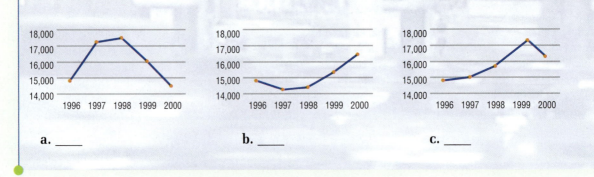

a. _____   b. _____   c. _____

2. Listen and fill in the blanks with words from the box.

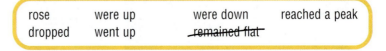

rose	were up	were down	reached a peak
dropped	went up	~~remained flat~~	

a. Sales _____*remained flat*_____ through 1997.

b. But in 1998, sales _____ steadily.

c. So in 1999, sales of the Coupe _____ dramatically.

d. At the end of that year, sales _____.

e. The next year, gas prices _____ and sales

_____.

f. In 2000, our figures _____ by 900 units.

NUMBERS

3. Listen to the sales manager's description again. Fill in the numbers.

TOTAL SALES 1996–2000: COUPE XL				
1996	1997	1998	1999	2000
14,900				

Listen again and check your answers.

SPEAKING

Sales reached a peak.

4. Speaker A, use this page. Speaker B, see the Activity File on page 89.

Speaker A, use the words in the box and describe the sales graph of the 450XG truck to Speaker B.

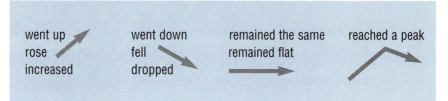

went up	went down	remained the same	reached a peak
rose	fell	remained flat	
increased	dropped		

Example

In 1996, sales remained flat at 14,500.
Then the figures went up/down to . . .

450XG Sales 1996 – 2002

5. Listen to Speaker B's description and complete the graph.

Conversation Strategies

Controlling the Flow of Information
- Just a minute.
- Can we back up a minute?
- Let me get that down.

350LG Sales 1996 – 2002

16,000

15,000

14,000

1996 1997 1998 1999 2000 2001 2002

6. Give reasons for the rising or falling sales on the graph in exercise 4. Use some of the reasons in the box or your own ideas.

> We ran an advertising campaign.
> We changed the price.
> We faced increasing competition.
> The customers didn't like the design.

Go to the extra speaking activity on page 94.

Raising the Titanic

1. Read the article.

Business Culture

When Fernando Pinto became CEO of Varig Airlines in January 1996, the job of turning the company around was compared to "raising the Titanic." The company was behind in every way, and employee morale was at an all-time low. Pinto's office did not even have a computer, just a typewriter.

Pinto immediately announced a plan to "revolutionize" the company. Focusing first on customer satisfaction, he gave bonuses to employees who met company goals of improved service. As a result, customer satisfaction improved from 80 to 95 percent during Pinto's first 18 months. To change the image of the company, he redesigned the old 1945 logo to a more modern-looking image. To increase Varig's profitability, Pinto had to sell aircraft, lay off 2,000 workers, and discontinue unprofitable routes. Finally, Pinto brought Varig into

the modern era by purchasing 5,500 new computers, and he invested $30 million in software programs to increase efficiency.

Although Varig continued to have problems, the turnaround was considered a success. In 1999, Pinto was elected "Businessman of the Year" by Brazil's National Commerce Federation. Varig also won the World Travel Award for the best airline in Latin America that year.

Source: Latin CEO

2. Match the beginnings and endings of the sentences according to the article.

_3_ **a.** In order to improve customer satisfaction,	**1.** so he discontinued some of them.
___ **b.** Pinto wanted to change the image of the company,	**2.** Pinto invested in new technology.
___ **c.** Because the company had financial difficulties,	**3.** Pinto gave bonuses to employees.
___ **d.** Varig's routes were unprofitable,	**4.** so he redesigned the logo.
___ **e.** In order to improve Varig's computer systems,	**5.** Pinto sold some of Varig's airplanes.

Talk About It

3. Look at the problems below. Discuss two possible ways to deal with each of the problems.

> increasing competition   low customer satisfaction
> low employee morale   bad public image

WRITING

A Business Report

4. Read the following report from a customer service manager of an airline.

GWB
A I R

Passenger Survey: Results

We identified the following areas of concern in this year's Passenger Survey:

1. Boarding was slow because passengers had to wait a long time while other passengers put away their luggage and settled into their seats.

2. Passengers missed connections to international flights because of delays at the check–in counter.

3. Passengers at the back of the plane could not see the screen during the in–flight entertainment.

We took the following action to deal with passengers' concerns.

Item 1

We introduced a system of boarding by zone on all of our routes. Passengers now board the plane according to a zone color on their boarding card. In addition, we now begin boarding 40 minutes before departure.

Result

In our Passenger Survey, the percentage of complaints about boarding time fell from 13 to 5 percent.

5. Choose item 2 or 3 from the survey above. Write a report about action taken and the results of the action.

Useful Language

- We required flight attendants to ____.
- We installed/ redesigned ____.
- We assigned more personnel to ____.
- As a result, ____.

Describing Processes

BUSINESS TALK

GETTING STARTED

Orange Juice: The Production Process

1

2

3

4

Source: Tropicana®

1. **Look at the pictures from a Tropicana® plant. Then number the steps below in the correct order.**

___ **a.** Then the juice is put into containers.

_1_ **b.** When the fruit is received at our plant, it is washed and sorted.

___ **c.** Next, the oranges are put into machines that remove the juice.

___ **d.** Finally, our juice is distributed all over the world.

🎧 **Listen and check your answers.**

2. **Describe four steps in the hiring process. Combine the words in the box and describe the steps.**

Example

First, the job position is advertised.

First . . .	the top candidates	are reviewed.
Next . . .	the best person	is advertised.
Then . . .	the job position	is offered the job.
Finally . . .	the résumés	are interviewed.

Go to page 103 for Summary Language

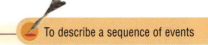
CONVERSATION

How does your system work?

🎧 **3.** Read and listen to the conversation.

How does your management training system work?

Well, we have a two-step process. Let me explain.

First, each employee is evaluated every year.

I see.

- are your managers selected for training
- Here's how it works.
- we review each employee

Then employees are ranked according to performance.

Really? How's that done?

It's done by a management team. The idea is to find and train future managers.

That's an interesting system.

- After that
- How do you do that?
- purpose
- process

🎧 Listen again and repeat.

4. Practice the conversation with a partner.

Pronunciation Focus: Linking

🎧 **5.** Listen and repeat.

a. Each employee is evaluated.
b. Then employees are ranked.
c. Future managers are selected for training.
d. That's an interesting system.

LISTENING

Customers rely on our company.

🎧 **1. A manager at UPS is explaining the delivery process. Listen and number the steps from 1–5.**

___ **a.** The package is unloaded, sorted, and put on a conveyor belt.

_1_ **b.** The package is picked up.

___ **c.** The package is taken off the conveyor belt, and loaded on a truck for local delivery.

___ **d.** The package is taken to a hub.

___ **e.** The package is taken to a local operating center.

2. Fill in the blanks with words from the box.

> double-checked   loaded   sorted   taken   ~~unloaded~~

At the hub, the package is carefully (a)___unloaded___, sorted by address, put on conveyor belts, and sent to the other end of the hub. Then the package is (b) _____ off the conveyor belt and (c) _____ on a truck or van for local delivery or for shipment elsewhere. Each package is always (d) _____ to make sure that it is (e)_____ correctly.

🎧 **Listen again and check your answers.**

NUMBERS

🎧 **3. Listen to the UPS manager. Fill in the numbers.**

Volume: approx. (a) _13.5_ *million packages and documents every day*
Truck Size: (b) _____ *to (c)* _____ *feet*
Capacity: up to (d) _____ *packages*
Drivers can deliver up to (e) _____ *packages daily*
Number of air packages: (f) _____ *each day*
To: (g) _____ *domestic airports*
To: (h) _____ *international airports*

Source: UPS

🎧 **Listen again and check your answers.**

SPEAKING

Two Ways to Buy Groceries

Conversation Strategies

Checking for Understanding
- ■ Do you want me to repeat that?
- ■ Do you have any questions?
- ■ Is that clear?

4. Speaker A, use this page. Speaker B, see the Activity File on page 90.

Speaker A, look at the steps involved in the traditional process in the flow chart below. Use the words in the box and describe the process to Speaker B.

First . . .   Then . . .   Next . . .   After that . . .   Finally . . .

Example

A: First, the supermarket places an order with the warehouse.

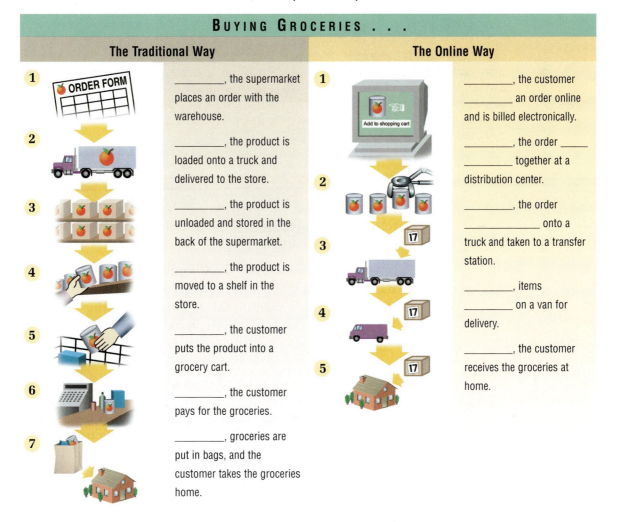

BUYING GROCERIES . . .

The Traditional Way

1 ORDER FORM

_____, the supermarket places an order with the warehouse.

2 _____, the product is loaded onto a truck and delivered to the store.

3 _____, the product is unloaded and stored in the back of the supermarket.

4 _____, the product is moved to a shelf in the store.

5 _____, the customer puts the product into a grocery cart.

6 _____, the customer pays for the groceries.

7 _____, groceries are put in bags, and the customer takes the groceries home.

The Online Way

1 Add to shopping cart

_____, the customer _____ an order online and is billed electronically.

2 _____, the order _____ _____ together at a distribution center.

3 17 _____, the order _____ onto a truck and taken to a transfer station.

4 17 _____, items _____ on a van for delivery.

5 17 _____, the customer receives the groceries at home.

5. Listen to Speaker B's description of the online buying process. Complete the sentences in the chart above.

6. Discuss the two processes. Which steps are eliminated or changed when customers buy online?

Go to the extra speaking activity on page 94.

READING

E-Commerce Is Here to Stay

1. Read the article.

Business Culture

The Internet is changing the way business is done worldwide. Everyone from property developers in Hong Kong to banks in Argentina is doing business online. In business–to–business (B2B) e-commerce, companies use the Internet to conduct business with each other. This offers tremendous opportunities for all types of businesses.

For smaller manufacturers and exporters, the Internet is an equalizer. It allows them to compete with much bigger businesses for buyers anywhere in the world, just for the cost of setting up and maintaining a website.

Today, most banks provide online services to businesses as well as to individual customers. Businesses can now complete bank transactions, such as collection and payments on the Web. This avoids an endless paper trail of invoices and receipts.

The Internet also gives manufacturers and suppliers greater access to each other. At TSMC, Taiwan's integrated circuit chip manufacturer, buyers use the Internet to check manufacturing schedules, inform the company when they need supplies, and follow the order process through the manufacturing cycle. At TSMC, the company can share important information with its suppliers, transmit orders, and even notify their salespeople on their pagers when an order is ready.

Source: Lexis/Nexis; Financial Times

2. Circle the ONE advantage of the Internet that is NOT mentioned in the article.

    a. Small companies can sell their products worldwide.
    b. Businesses can do banking transactions online.
    c. Buyers can check manufacturing schedules online.
    d. Large retailers can sell directly to the customer.
    e. Buyers can check the status of their orders online.

Talk About It

3. How does your company (or a company that you know) use the Internet? For example, consider the following uses:

- internal communication
- communication with offices in other countries
- a website with company information
- a website with goods to purchase
- research

WRITING

E-mail Replies to Customers

4. Read the following e-mails.

To: poliveira@metrosystems.com.br
Date: Monday, February 28, 2001
Subject: Order 3076-01

Ms. Oliveira:

We have received shipment on our order 3076-01 and it is incomplete. The order included 750 Type 3 cylinders. These are missing from the shipment.

Please let us know the status of the cylinders.
Thank you.

YW Lee

To: ywlee@kortek.com.kr
Date: Monday, February 28, 2001
Subject: Order 3076-01

Dear Mr. Lee:

I checked the status of your order (#3076-01). The order was not complete because item 27780005X (750 Type 3 cylinders) was out of stock at the time your order was received.

The cylinders were shipped on Feb 25 and will arrive in Pusan on March 14.

Please feel free to contact me if you have further questions.

Paula Oliveira

5. Read the e-mail below and write a reply.

Useful Language

- The items are back ordered/out of stock/ready for shipment.
- The order was shipped this morning/incorrectly addressed/refused by customs.

To: manager@suppliesplus.com.
Date: Monday, March 29, 2001
Subject: Order 30002-7764

In our order of March 7, #300027764, the following items were not delivered:

Item # 9773: steel frames (quantity: 250)
Item # 8650: sockets (quantity: 2000)

Please let us know when we can expect delivery. Thank you.

Jonathan Koh

Teamwork

BUSINESS TALK

GETTING STARTED

1. Look at the picture.

Match each sentence or question above with the correct response.

___ **a.** Yes, please.
___ **b.** No problem.
___ **c.** Yes. Why don't we go now?

🎧 Listen and check your answers.

2. Work with a partner. Speaker A, make a request, offer, or suggestion from Box A. Speaker B, answer using a response from Box B. Take turns.

Example

A: Should I schedule the presentation?
B: That's a good idea.

A		B
a. Should I	schedule the presentation?	OK.
b. Could you	work out a schedule?	That would be great.
c. Would you	write an e-mail?	That's a good idea.
d. Why don't we	put off the meeting?	No problem.
		Of course.
		Yes, please.

Go to page 104 for Summary Language

CONVERSATION

Would you mind calling Alan?

🎧 **3.** Read and listen to the conversation.

Would you mind calling Alan when you get a chance? We ought to ask him about the production schedule.

No problem. I'll call him later this morning.

May I borrow your copy of the schedule?

Sure. So, what **do you want to** do about the production meeting tomorrow?

• Could you call   • OK.   • Could I use   • should we

I think that's the best thing to do. **Should I e-mail everyone?**

Oh, I forgot all about it. **Let's postpone it for now.**

Yes, please. And send a copy to Alan.

OK.

• Why don't we put it off for the moment?   • I'll e-mail the team.   • That would be great.   • I'll do that.

🎧 Listen again and repeat.

4. Practice the conversation with a partner.

Pronunciation Focus: Requests and offers

🎧 **5.** Listen and repeat.

     a. Would you mind calling Alan?

     b. May I borrow your copy of the schedule?

     c. Should I e-mail everyone?

LISTENING

Are we ready for the trade fair?

🎧 **1.** Jerry Marks, Diane Atkinson, and Luis Borrego are executives. They are discussing preparations for a trade fair.

Look at the items below. Then listen and check (✔) the four items they discuss.

✔ **a.** location of the booth
___ **b.** equipment at the booth
___ **c.** hotel accommodations
___ **d.** transportation to the conference center
___ **e.** staffing the booth
___ **f.** product demonstrations
___ **g.** promotional brochures
___ **h.** special events

🎧 **2.** Listen again. Complete the sentences in your own words.

a. Diane is going to find out about _____ .

b. Luis is going to work out _____ .

c. Jerry is going to talk to Tom about _____ .

SPEAKING

Last-Minute Problems

Conversation Strategies

Expressing Reluctance
- Hmm. I'm not sure that's possible.
- That might be a bit difficult.

3. Work with a partner. You work for a telecommunications company that is exhibiting at a trade fair in Miami.

Speaker A, you are in charge of marketing. Speaker B, you are the person in contact with the conference center. Read your messages. What should each person do? Make suggestions. Use the words in the box and your own ideas.

> Could you…?   Let's (ask)…
> Should I…?   Why don't you/we….
> We should/ought to…   Would you mind ___-ing…?

Example

A: *What should we do about the message from George?*
B: *Well, I could talk to …*

Message from George Taylor

My travel plans have changed. I can't make it to Miami until Thursday. Can you change the meeting with the sales team from Wednesday to Thursday? Also, could someone give me an idea of the cost of the reception we're holding on Friday? It is Friday, right?

George

Change meeting room reservation, too!

From: Sylvia Tan
Sent: May 11, 1:46 p.m.
Subject: Brochures

Greetings from the Convention Center. I checked the status of our brochures. There's a problem with the local delivery service, and the brochures may not arrive until Thursday. Can you bring enough with you to cover the first day or two?

Also, I think we ought to have the Spanish version of our promotional videos available at the booth. Could you look into this?

Date: May 12, 7:30 a.m.
From: Miami Accommodations Center 1-305-987-4321

Message:
No more rooms available at the Conference Center Hotel for 5/13-5/16. They can book your sales rep John Koh into a room at the Classic Hotel, three miles across town. There are some shared suites available at the Conference Center. Would John be willing to share? Please let them know ASAP. Ask for Ruben.

Go to the extra speaking activity on page 95.

Information Overload

1. Read the article.

Business Culture

There's the fax, voice mail, and e-mail. Then there's the telephone, the cell phone, the car phone, and the pager.

A recent study found that workers receive an astonishing number of messages from computerized devices. Employees who were surveyed received an average of 190 messages each day. Most of the messages require some form of response. Forty percent of the workers said they are interrupted by incoming messages six or more times an hour.

Economist Paula Rayman, director of the Radcliffe Public Policy Institute, said that people are frustrated because they are working longer hours to handle all the requests for information and communication. "People are treated like they are machines that are on all the time," she said.

Many experts believe that the growth of information technology is making people work more efficiently. But not everybody agrees that it has a positive effect on productivity. New technology eliminates some of the old, boring tasks and gives many more people access to data. But workers need to learn to manage the flow of information. For example, they need to be strict about deleting unnecessary telephone messages and moving unimportant e-mail straight to the trash.

Employees also need strategies to deal with interruptions. As Rayman points out, "If you are constantly bombarded with messages, you never get your real work done."

SURVEY RESULTS	
Telephone, pager, cell phone: 59	Fax: 15
E-mail: 30	Telephone messages, notes: 21
Voice mail: 22	Courier/express mail: 7
Regular and interoffice mail: 36	
Average number of messages daily: 190	

Source: Salt Lake Tribune/Washington Post

2. Answer the questions.

a. What problem is described in the article?

b. What has caused this problem?

c. According to the article, what should workers do to overcome the problem?

Talk About It

3. Discuss the questions.

a. What means of communication do you use the most? The telephone, e-mail, letters, or memos? Why?

b. What do you do to avoid interruptions at work?

c. What kind of correspondence should not be sent via e-mail? Why? Do you think this is different in other countries?

NUMBERS

4. Work with a partner. Look at the results of the survey in Exercise 1. Discuss how this compares with your daily communication.

Example

I get about 20 telephone calls a day. The average in the survey was 59.

WRITING

A Memo to Managers

5. Read the memo.

MEMO

Date: May 3, 2001
To: Tom Cook
From: Robert Stone
RE: Monthly Reports

Thank you all for turning in your monthly reports on time. I realize the reports are time-consuming to write, but the information you provide is very useful in managing projects.

Here are a few guidelines for next month's report. Please remember not to use formatting when writing these reports. In other words, no **boldface**, no <u>underlining</u>, no *italics*, and no bullet points (•). Also, if possible, could you please use a 12-point font size?

Thank you.

You work in the purchasing department of a large company. Write a memo to managers describing a new system for ordering computers. Include the following points:

a. Do not place orders by voice mail. Use e–mail instead.

b. Include the model number and description for each item.

c. Include employee ID number and department on all orders.

Useful Language

- Please remember to _____.
- If possible, could you please _____.
- May I remind you not to _____.

Managing Change

BUSINESS TALK

GETTING STARTED

1. Read the headlines. Match each of the headlines with the sentences below.

a CPC Posts Record Profit

b CPC Sales Down 35%

c CPC STOCK UP 42%

d 2,000 Layoffs in CPC Restructuring

e CPC LAUNCHES NEW PRODUCT LINE

f CPC Finds New Leader

_b_ **1.** Sales have fallen sharply.
___ **2.** The company has appointed a new CEO.
___ **3.** They have laid off a lot of workers.
___ **4.** They have introduced new products.
___ **5.** They've made a profit.
___ **6.** Stock prices have gone up.

2. Work with a partner. Talk about your company or a company that has been in the news recently. What changes have happened? Use the words in the box or ideas of your own.

We have (Company X) has	introduced appointed begun work on/started restructured	a new product/new software. a new manager/a new CEO. the ___ project/a new building. a ___ system. the marketing division.

OBJECTIVES

■ To describe changes at a company

■ To describe a company's past and present performance

■ To write a report describing recent achievements

Go to page 105 for Summary Language

CONVERSATION

We've restructured the company.

3. Read and listen to the conversation.

I hear your company has **reorganized** recently.

We certainly have. We've restructured the company into three divisions.

• made some changes

That's quite a change.

Yes, and we've **changed** our distribution channels. We're only using 12 distributors now.

• reduced

Really?

And instead of doing our own **hiring, we're using professional recruiters.**

• recruiting, we've hired an outside company

That way we can concentrate on expanding our **services.**

It sounds like **you're on the right track.**

• product line

• a good idea

Listen again and repeat.

4. Practice the conversation with a partner.

Pronunciation Focus: Linking after *–ed* endings

5. Listen and repeat.

  a. We've changed our distribution channels.
  b. We've hired an outside company.
  c. We've introduced a new product.
  d. We've appointed a new manager.

LISTENING

An End-of-Year Presentation

🎧 **1.** The CEO of Western Air is giving an end-of-year presentation. Listen and choose the correct ending for each sentence.

a. The airline is doing ___.
  1. better than last year
  2. as well as last year
  3. worse than last year

b. They have developed ___ .
  1. a new airplane design
  2. an extensive training program
  3. a new airport in Singapore

c. Customer service complaints have ___.
  1. dropped
  2. not changed
  3. increased

🎧 **2.** Listen again. Circle the correct choice.

a. The company's market share has (increased)/decreased.
b. They have received *35/15* new planes.
c. They have trained *more than half/less than half* of the pilots and mechanics.
d. They have *reduced/extended* service on the Singapore route.

NUMBERS

🎧 **3.** Listen to the end of the presentation. Fill in the blanks with numbers and percentages.

	Number or percentage this year	Percent increase/decrease
Complaints	$7\frac{1}{2}$ %	-50%
Passengers		
Passengers (August)		
Cargo		

🎧 Listen again and check your answers.

SPEAKING

Have their sales increased this year?

4. Work with a partner. Read the information. Pen and Paper, a large retailer of office supplies and equipment, is for sale. This year the company invested in developing a website and is now selling products online. Your company is thinking of buying it.

Look at the chart. Discuss how the company has performed.

Example

A: *Sales have fallen from 7.2 billion dollars last year to 4.4 billion this year.*

B: *That's quite a change. They've also lost market share. Last year. . .*

PEN AND PAPER: TWO-YEAR-PERFORMANCE		
	Last year	**This year**
Sales figures	$7.2B	$4.4B
Market share	48%	37%
Stores opened	120	60
Products offered (stores)	12,000	7,000
Products offered (online)	——	15,000
Distribution centers	3	5
Employees hired	300 (sales people)	100 (technical workers)
Profit	$60M	$46M
Earnings per share	92 cents	50 cents

5. Discuss the questions.

a. What do you think will happen to Pen and Paper in the future?

b. Should your company buy Pen and Paper?

Conversation Strategies

Summing Up
- So, basically _____.
- What I'm saying is _____.
- So, overall _____.

Go to the extra speaking activity on page 95.

READING

Strategic Outsourcing

1. Read the article.

Business Culture

Nowadays more and more companies are outsourcing parts of their operations in order to become more flexible in a changing business environment. In the practice of outsourcing, companies hire outside businesses to handle parts of their internal operations. In the past decade, outsourcing has helped many companies focus on the most important parts of their business: growth and profitability.

Companies such as General Electric, Nike, Xerox, and Microsoft use outsourcing in different ways. Organizations have outsourced such functions as information technology, real estate management, human resources, and finance.

A big advantage of outsourcing is that it allows an enterprise to concentrate on the business it does best. For example, a bank may outsource its real estate management, but it would never outsource the core of its business: financial transactions. Of course, before contracting out internal functions, a company must first carefully examine which processes are less essential.

Source: Management Review

2. Answer the questions.

   a. What is outsourcing? Find a definition in the article.
   b. Why do companies use outsourcing?
   c. What types of functions are often outsourced?

Talk About It

3. Look at the list of functions in the box. Discuss which functions might be outsourced by a bank, a telecommunications company, and an airline.

food preparation	information technology	maintenance services
human resources	real estate management	security services

WRITING

An Annual Report

4. Read the report.

CPC, Inc.

ANNUAL REPORT

This year has been a very successful year for CPC. This report focuses on three key achievements:

1 The introduction of our new line of medical equipment has been very successful. We expect a steady increase in sales next year.

2 We have restructured our distribution system by signing an agreement with Thomson Transport for transportation and distribution.

3 Our stock price has gone up 15 percent since last year.

Decide on the three most important achievements in your company or your department over the last 12 months. (As an alternative, consider the achievements of Western Air or Pen and Paper discussed earlier in this unit.) Write a short report highlighting these achievements.

Useful Language

■ We have restructured/reorganized/changed/started _____.
■ We are continuing to work on/improve/expand _____.

Clients and Customers

BUSINESS TALK

GETTING STARTED

1. Read the advertisement.

1 "Last month we didn't have enough inventory. Now we have too much!"

2 "We need more technical support. Too many customers are waiting too long on our help line."

3 "Marketing isn't getting enough customer feedback."

Do these problems sound familiar?
Converge Software helps you plan your inventory, meet customers' needs, and improve communication systems.
No more embarrassing apologies!

2. Circle the expression that describes each situation above.

a. Situation 1: *too many/not enough* items in stock
b. Situation 2: *too much/not enough* technical support
c. Situation 3: *too much/not enough* customer feedback

3. Work with a partner. Talk about business problems. Use the words in the box and your own ideas.

Examples

*Sometimes, there is too much/
there are too many . . .*
Usually, we have a lot of . . .
We never have enough . . .

BUSINESS PROBLEMS

competition
complaints
feedback
inventory
space
technical support
time

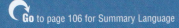

Go to page 106 for Summary Language

CONVERSATION

It's taking too long.

4. **Read and listen to the conversation.**

- How can I help you
- too much time
- you've been waiting so long
- our inventory is low
- Here's what I'll do.
- help
- Yes.

Listen again and repeat.

5. **Practice the conversation with a partner.**

Pronunciation Focus: Stress

6. **Listen and repeat.**

  a. It's taking too long.
  b. I'll tell you what.
  c. I'd appreciate it.

LISTENING

Doing OK is not enough.

🎧 **1.** A management consultant is speaking at a training seminar. Listen. Circle the main topic of the talk.

    a. using complaint forms for customer feedback

    b. getting information from your customers

    c. managing customer service representatives

🎧 **2.** Listen again. Circle the correct answer to each question.

    a. What is a common way of getting feedback from customers?
        1. talking to distributors
        2. visiting customers' homes
        3. complaint forms

    b. Who else, besides customers, can provide useful feedback?
        1. project managers
        2. sales representatives
        3. telecommunications companies

    c. What should managers do with the feedback they receive?
        1. Organize data and distribute it to the appropriate staff.
        2. Talk with customers about it.
        3. Give the feedback to distributors.

    d. How did Intuit get more feedback from their customers?
        1. They installed the software for them.
        2. They observed customers installing new software at home.
        3. They had representatives ask customers many questions.

SPEAKING

I'm calling about the pagers.

3. Speaker A, use this page. Speaker B, see the Activity File on page 91.

Speaker A, read Situation 1 and follow the instructions.

SITUATION 1

Speaker A, you are the general manager of a transportation company. You ordered 40 new pagers for your drivers last month, but they still have not arrived. The old pagers are not powerful enough, and your drivers are missing calls. You've had too many customer complaints, and you need the pagers as soon as possible.

Speaker B is the sales manager at the pager company. Call him or her and explain the situation.

Example

A: *I'm calling about our order. We haven't received the pagers.*
B: *I'm sorry for the delay. Unfortunately,….*

4. Read Situation 2 and follow the instructions.

Conversation Strategies

Ending a Conversation by Promising Action

■ OK. I'll tell you what. I'll _____.

■ Anyway, why don't I _____?

■ All right. Let me discuss this with _____, and I'll get back to you.

SITUATION 2

You are the project manager for a software firm. Your team is installing a new software system for a large company. You have been working on the project for a month, and things are going well. You need a few more software engineers because the project is a little behind schedule. With more engineers you could finish the project in a week.

Speaker B is one of the senior managers of the company and wants to speak to you. Listen and suggest a way of solving the problem.

Example

B: *How's the software project going? We need to know how much longer it will take.*
A: *The project is going well…*

Go to the extra speaking activity on page 95.

READING

Quality Means Service, Too

1. Read the article.

Business Culture

In the past, quality control was seen primarily as a manufacturing problem. But what makes a company stand out today is the quality of the service it provides to the customer. This has encouraged the trend towards total quality management, or TQM.

TQM has redefined quality to mean "what feels right to the customer." For Ford, that means a toll–free number to respond to customer complaints quickly. For Federal Express, it means an online tracking system that allows customers to know where their packages are at any time. For IBM, it's a system that automatically recognizes trouble and alerts technicians—sometimes before the clients know they have a problem.

From the customer's perspective, everything has to run smoothly—from technical support to personal service. Hotel clerks may be polite and attentive, but if the computer system is down, their politeness isn't going to be enough. The aim of total quality management is to get everyone working together, while keeping the customer in focus.

A serious TQM effort requires a considerable investment in training, consultants, and—most difficult of all—top management attention. But some CEOs, like Fred Smith of Federal Express, are obsessive on the subject of quality. "It really has to be the be–all and end–all," Smith declares.

Source: Fortune

2. Check (✓) the ideas that are included in the article.

___ **a.** Quality control is more important than quality of service.

___ **b.** TQM focuses on the customer.

___ **c.** Ford, Federal Express, and IBM are committed to quality.

___ **d.** TQM involves all the parts of an organization working together.

___ **e.** TQM is often cheaper in the long run.

___ **f.** Not all CEOs are interested in TQM.

Talk About It

3. Discuss the following questions.

a. Describe a personal experience of good or bad service from one of the following:

an airline   an automobile manufacturer   a bank   a hotel

b. Discuss how your company (or one you know about) could improve service to its customers or clients.

c. How do the attitudes toward customer service differ in different countries or industries?

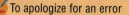
WRITING

An Apology

4. Read the e–mail.

```
To:      sueb@llama.net
Sent:    July 6, 1:02 p.m.
From:    mcipriani@dwc.com
Subject: Invoice G45002

Thank you for your e-mail regarding the error on our
last invoice (# G45002). There was an administrative
error on our part. We have corrected our records and
are sending you a new invoice for $9,679.50.

I hope this resolves the issue to your satisfaction.
Please accept our apologies for any inconvenience.

Maria Cipriani
```

Useful Language

- Please accept our apologies for any inconvenience.
- I've checked your account carefully and ___.
- Unfortunately, due to ___.

Write an e–mail in response to the message below. Include an apology.

```
To:   mcipriani@dwc.com
Sent: Sept.6, 9:05 a.m.
From: pff@unifix.com
Re:   Invoice M55519

We've just received your invoice (M55519) for the
amount of $5,000, due on Sept. 10. I've checked with
our accounting department and found that the amount of
our last order (X52218), dated Aug. 8, was $3598.00.
Would you please look into this matter and get back to
me?

Patricia Franco
```

NUMBERS

5. Listen to the voice mail message. Correct the figures on the invoices.

Invoice No.	Amount	Invoice No.	Amount
5464	980 $~~890~~.45	5467	$413.18
5465	$1,462.90	5468	$670.00
5466	$790.50	5469	$4,430.50

Check your answers with a partner. Say the numbers.

Corporate Goals

BUSINESS TALK

GETTING STARTED

1. Three managers at a telecommunications company are speaking at a year-end meeting. Read and listen to the quotes from their speeches. Then match the quotes with the managers.

1. Executive Manager, Finance

2. General Manager, International Division

3. Manager, Product Development

___3___ a. "We aim to develop cutting-edge technologies to support Internet communications."

_____ b. "We should maintain our strong financial position into the next decade."

_____ c. "We might also consider joint ventures with overseas Internet companies."

_____ d. "We expect to remain focused on developing e-commerce products."

_____ e. "We plan to introduce new services for our overseas clients next year."

2. Answer the questions.

a. Which two statements describe the company's goals or plans? ___*a*___ _____

b. Which one describes something that is only a possibility? _____

c. Which two statements above describe something that will probably happen? _____ _____

3. Work with a partner. Discuss the future activities of your company or a company that you know. Use some of the phrases from the box.

We aim to	expand service to . . .
We plan to	continue to work on . . .
We (don't) expect to	introduce a new . . .
We should	reach our sales . . .
We might (not)	begin a joint venture with . . .

OBJECTIVES

▪ To discuss business plans and expectations

▪ To prepare a business plan

▪ To describe department goals

Go to page 107 for Summary Language

CONVERSATION

What's going to happen?

🎧 **4.** Read and listen to the conversation.

We're going to introduce a new phone service plan next month.

Really? What's happening to the Phonelink plan?

• launch   • going to happen

We'll continue to offer it to residential customers. This new plan is just for corporate clients.

Hmm. How will it benefit them?

• We're going to continue it for   • What are the benefits?

We expect to reduce their telephone charges by about 20 percent.

That's great. It should be pretty popular.

• It should   • That sounds good.

Do you plan to reduce the rates for residential customers?

Maybe. And we might lower international rates.

• Are you going   • we're thinking of lowering

🎧 Listen again and repeat.

5. Practice the conversation with a partner.

Pronunciation **F**ocus: Unstressed *to*

🎧 **6.** Listen and repeat.

    a. We're going to introduce a new service plan.

    b. We'll continue to offer it to residential customers.

    c. We expect to reduce their phone charges.

LISTENING

We're pretty small right now.

1. **Read the questions. Then listen to the interview with Tony Chan of IT Systems and answer the questions.**

   a. What does Tony's company do? _____

   _____

   b. Where do most of his clients come from? Why?

   _____

   c. What are some of the plans that Tony has for the future?

   _____

2. **Listen. Circle the correct choice.**

   a. Tony ____ move into new markets.
   (hopes to)   isn't going to

   b. He ____ visit Taiwan, Korea, and Japan in February.
   might   plans to

   c. He ____ open an office in Japan.
   expects to   might

   d. He ____ travel a lot in the next few years.
   expects to   doesn't expect to

   e. He ____ expand the company's range of services.
   might   is going to

   f. The company ____ become a public company, selling shares to investors.
   will probably   is going to

3. **Listen. Pay attention to the underlined expressions in the sentences below.**

   _5_ **a.** So far, we get most of our business <u>by word of mouth</u>.

   ___ **b.** We hope to keep building our <u>client base</u>.

   ___ **c.** I wouldn't <u>rule that out</u>.

   ___ **d.** We'll probably <u>go public first</u>.

   ___ **e.** So that's <u>in the cards</u>?

   Now match the underlined expressions with the phrases below.

   1. probably going to happen
   2. number of clients
   3. allow the public to buy shares in the company
   4. say it's impossible
   5. from personal contacts

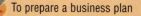

SPEAKING

Investing in a Business

4. Work with a partner. Your company is planning to invest in one of these businesses. Read the company profiles and decide which business to invest in.

Print and Photo Services
- **Services:** photocopying, high speed copying, design services, basic film and photo processing.
- **Location:** Good location in downtown area with a lot of walk-in customers.
- **Sales/Client Base:** Sales have fallen as more people do their own desktop publishing and digital photo processing. The business needs to expand its range of services to attract new customers and target marketing toward business customers.

Translation and Interpretation Services
- **Services:** document translation, live interpretation, mainly in the medical and manufacturing fields.
- **Location:** Office in downtown area.
- **Sales/Client Base:** Well-established language services for business clients. Company has about 50 long-term clients but needs to build its client base and possibly offer more services.

Conversation Strategies

Asking for an Opinion
- What do you think about ___?
- Would you agree that we should ___?
- Do you think it's a good idea to ___?

5. Discuss ways to expand the business. Then complete the business plan below and add your own ideas.

Example

A: I think we should expand the range of services.
B: I agree. Why don't we...?

Business Plan Worksheet

a. Range of Services (Check one.)
❏ Maintain ❏ Reduce ❏ Expand range of services
❏ Possible new services: _____
_____

b. Location (Check one or two.)
❏ Stay in same location ❏ Move to new location
❏ Open new branches in other locations

c. Investment (Check top two priorities.)
❏ Training and personnel ❏ Equipment ❏ Advertising
❏ Other: _____

d. Advertising (Check top choice.)
❏ Website ❏ Newspaper ❏ Direct mail ❏ Television
❏ Other: _____

Go to the extra speaking activity on page 96.

READING

Preparing for Group Presentations

1. Read the article.

Business Culture

Whether you're introducing a new company to investors or updating management on an important project, a well-planned presentation will make you look good. Presenting as a group is challenging. Here are some guidelines for planning and presenting as a team.

- **Develop outlines.** For each section of the presentation, identify key points to make.
- **Focus on clarity.** In general, simpler is better.
- **Plan your time well.** Allow enough time for each speaker and for questions at the end.
- **Put background information or data on a separate handout.** This will help listeners focus on your key points.
- **Remember your listeners' needs.** How long will people be sitting? You may decide to stop and take a break in the presentation at a mid-point.
- **Use visuals.** Visuals add variety to a presentation. But don't use too many, and avoid turning down the lights for too long, especially after lunch!
- **Practice the presentation as a team several times.** Each member needs to be familiar with everyone else's content. Pay attention to transition points. For example, how will a presenter introduce the next speaker?
- **Plan to arrive early and check your equipment.** Make sure that video screens and projectors are well-placed, plugged in, and working.

Source: San Francisco Examiner

2. Complete the following advice to a presenter, using one idea from the article in each sentence.

a. You won't have much time for your presentation, so ___*identify your key points*___ .

b. The audience will probably have questions, so _____ .

c. You have a lot of data to present, so _____ .

d. Your presentation is quite long, so _____ .

e. Four people are making the presentation, so _____ .

f. You plan to use a video, so_____ .

Talk About It

3. Discuss the questions.

a. What are three characteristics of a good business presentation?

b. What do you think is the most important advice in the article?

c. What advice would you give to a visitor from overseas who is making a presentation to your company? Consider dress, eye contact, length of presentation, visuals, and answering questions.

WRITING

A Report on Department Goals

4. Read the following excerpt taken from a department report.

We have identified the following goals for next year:

- **To expand into new markets.** We plan to expand our operations in Latin America next year.

- **To excel in service to our customers.** In February, we are putting in place a new system for handling customer complaints.

- **To maximize productivity.** We expect to install more efficient equipment in our factories.

Useful Language

- To achieve our goal, we will ___.
- To compete effectively, we will ___.

Write a report outlining two or three of your company's or department's goals for the future. Use some of the words in the box.

increase	expand	design
develop	start	improve
continue	launch	invest

NUMBERS

5. A sales manager is giving estimated sales forecasts. Listen and write the numbers that you hear. Use the abbreviation "K" for thousand.

Sales Forecasts for Video Monitors

MODEL	THIS YEAR	NEXT YEAR
XA1	250K	Between _____ and _____
XA2	_____	No more than _____
XB1	_____	_____ to _____
XB2	_____	At least _____

Check your answers with a partner. Say the numbers.

Describing and Comparing Products

OBJECTIVES

- To describe and compare product features

- To ask for information and compare products

- To write a memo describing features of a new product

BUSINESS TALK

GETTING STARTED

1. Look at the pictures and read the product descriptions.

The smallest telephone . . .
the tiniest movie theater imaginable . . .
a phone that does so much more . . .

Here are just a few of the hottest sellers!

1 This combination watch phone has a touch-tone dial and a tiny microphone/speaker. It rings when a call comes in. Push a button on the watch to talk. Weighs only one ounce more than a sport watch.

2 Inside this video headset a one-centimeter video screen shows movies while you listen to stereo sound from tiny speakers in your ears. Connects to a portable DVD player. Watch movies without disturbing anyone. Much better sound and vision than airline movies.

3 This smart phone is one of the most compact on the market. It can hold up to 1,000 contact names. Use it as a wireless modem for sending faxes and connecting to the Internet from your laptop.

2. Write the number of the product described.

___ **a.** provides better quality sound and vision than airline movies

___ **b.** is not much heavier than a regular watch

___ **c.** is one of the most compact on the market

3. Work with a partner. Describe a product that you are familiar with. Use some of the phrases from the box.

> It's faster/smaller/cheaper/easier to use than . . .
> It's more useful/compact/stylish than . . .
> It has more power/memory/features than . . .
> It's one of the fastest/most useful/most convenient ___ on the market.

Go to page 108 for Summary Language

CONVERSATION

It's a better product.

4. Read and listen to the conversation.

I think you all know about our **newest** product, the Telec digital cell phone . . .

Yes, but how **does the Telec compare to** our biggest competitor, the Portacall 100?

Good question, Joe. Well, it's much lighter and slimmer. And the battery lasts longer.

There's a lot of **demand for** something like that.

And it's a better product. It uses the latest technology.

Is it competitively priced?

It's a little more expensive than the Portacall. But we're offering better discounts.

That's good. **The competition gets tougher every year.**

- latest
- is the Telec different from
- Our customers are always looking for
- How does it compare price-wise?
- It's a very competitive market.

Listen again and repeat.

5. Practice the conversation with a partner.

Pronunciation Focus: Stress with comparative forms

6. Listen and repeat.

a. That's our biggest competitor.
b. It's much lighter and slimmer.
c. It's a better product.
d. It's a little more expensive.

LISTENING

What does it do?

🎧 **1.** Look at the items below. Then listen to the conversation. Check (✓) the two items that the salesperson describes.

a. _____

b. _____

c. _____

🎧 **2.** Listen again and complete the chart.

	First Product	Second Product
Modem	External	_____
Data Input	_____	Keyboard
Memory (RAM)	_____ megabytes	_____ megabytes
Size	▰▰▰▰▰	_____ inches
Weight	_____ ounces	_____ pound(s)
Battery Life	_____ hours	▰▰▰▰▰

🎧 **3.** Listen. Write the questions that the buyer asks about each of the following features.

    a. Modem: _____ *Is there a modem?* _____

    b. Data input: _____

    c. Memory: _____

    d. Weight: _____

    e. Battery life: _____

NUMBERS

ABBREVIATIONS

MB = megabyte(s)
lb = pound(s)
oz = ounce(s)
cm = centimeter(s)
kg = kilogram(s)
in = inch(es)
hr = hour(s)
mo = months
yr = year(s)

🎧 **4.** Listen to the salesperson and fill in the product specifications for the laptop computer.

    a. RAM: _____ MB

    b. Weight: _____ lb (_____ kg)

    c. Screen: _____ in (_____ cm)

    d. Warranty: _____ mo

🎧 Listen again and check your answers.

SPEAKING

How do they compare?

5. Speaker A, use this page. Speaker B, see the Activity File on page 92.

Speaker A, ask Speaker B for information about the PQ 5 and fill in the chart. Use the words in the box.

> How much . . . ?   How big . . . ?   How long . . . ?   Is there . . . ?

Example

A: *How much does the PQ 5 cost?*
B: *It's $2,163 dollars.*

Model	PQ 5	NS 3
Price	$2,163	$1,521
Memory (RAM)		32 MB
Screen Size		13.3 in
Internal Modem		yes
Battery Life		3 hr
Weight		6.7 lb
Technical Support		Free phone support for 3 yr

Conversation Strategies

Correcting Information
- Actually, it's not fifty-three. It's sixty-three.
- Sorry. I meant to say three hours, not six.
- No, there is an internal modem.

6. Look at the information about the NS 3 and answer Speaker B's questions.

7. Compare the two laptops. What are the main differences? Which do you prefer? Use the words in the box and your own ideas.

> It's faster/smaller/cheaper/more useful than . . .
> It has more power/memory/features than . . .

Go to the extra speaking activity on page 96.

READING

Sometimes Honesty Is the Best Policy

1. Read the article.

Business Culture

In more than 40 years as a salesperson, Jacques Werth has accomplished at least two things: He's made a lot of money and learned a lot about sales, enough to write a book entitled *High Probability Selling*. Werth's view of selling is simple but unusual: just be honest. The following is from an interview with Werth.

Q: What is the biggest mistake that salespeople make?

A: Most people think that it's important to be aggressive in sales, but the opposite is true. Aggressive people are too pushy. They try to persuade people—to convince them to buy.

Q: Why? Aren't salespeople supposed to persuade people?

A: Most people dislike being persuaded. It's much better to find consumers who want to buy your product and arrive at an agreement that makes everybody happy.

Q: How do you do that?

A: You find out quickly who isn't going to buy your product and move on. People may be interested, but they're not necessarily going to buy. They just waste your time.

Q: So what kind of person makes the best salesperson?

A: Honest people who will listen to the customer and tell the truth.

Source: Entrepreneur Magazine

2. Check (✓) *yes* or *no* according to the advice in the article.

	YES	NO
a. Be aggressive.	☐	☑
b. Persuade the customer that he/she needs the product.	☐	☐
c. Quickly identify the customers who are ready to buy.	☐	☐
d. Spend time with people who are interested in your product.	☐	☐
e. Listen to the customer.	☐	☐

Talk About It

3. Discuss the questions.

a. What do you think of the advice in the article? In sales, is honesty always the best policy?

b. What do salespeople do to persuade people to buy their products? Are they effective?

c. What advice would you give to a salesperson who wants to succeed in your country or in your industry?

WRITING

Memo to Sales Staff

4. Look at the memo.

To: Sales Personnel
From: Rob White
Date: April 4, 2001

Subject: GYX 24 launch

In response to customer demand,
we are introducing the GYX 24,
our biggest flat-panel computer monitor,
next month.

THE GYX 24:

• a completely flat 24-inch screen: no distortion
• the lightest monitor on the market

Please emphasize these features to our customers.

Useful Language

■ In response to customer demand, we are introducing ___.

■ Please emphasize these features to our customers/clients/sales force.

Write a memo to your sales staff about the digital camera below. Read the notes, choose two important features, and describe them.

Pocketpix II Digital Camera
Launch date: May

Features
Compact: fits in a pocket
Uses a standard floppy disk
4X zoom lens: the most powerful on the market
Longer battery life than most cameras
Weighs only 8.8oz

Challenges to Management

BUSINESS TALK

GETTING STARTED

OBJECTIVES

■ To describe project and staffing difficulties

■ To discuss and compare employee benefits

■ To summarize the main points of a meeting

1. Bob Congdon is a project manager at a software company. Listen to Bob's three voice-mail messages. Circle the correct choice.

   a. David *has to*/*needs to* have your sales figures by the end of the day.
   b. If you can't do it, maybe Maria *will*/*can* help.
   c. I *can*/*can't* come to the meeting this morning.
   d. I *have to*/*had to* change my flight because I got delayed at the plant.
   e. I think *we'll have to*/*we'll need to* get some more people on it.
   f. Otherwise, we *can't*/*won't* be able to meet the deadline.

2. Work with a partner. Talk about your work obligations. Use the words in the box.

> On Tuesday, I have to . . .   Next month, we'll probably have to . . .
> I don't usually have to . . .   We often need to . . .
> Tomorrow I won't be able to . . .

Example

I usually have to attend three or four meetings a week.

WORK OBLIGATIONS

attend meetings
travel on short notice
meet deadlines
write monthly reports
prepare sales figures

Go to page 109 for Summary Language

CONVERSATION

We won't be able to meet the deadline.

🎧 **3.** Read and listen to the conversation.

How's the Unex project going?

Well, I'm afraid we're behind schedule. We're very short-staffed.

- What's the status of the Unex project?
- We don't have enough people.

Can't you hire some more people?

That's easier said than done. They have to have the right skills.

- need to be familiar with this type of project

I see your point. Maybe we can reassign some people from Jay's project.

I'd rather not do that. His project's behind too.

- That makes sense.
- I don't really want to

But we don't have a choice. We won't be able to meet the deadline otherwise.

I guess you're right. Unex is a top priority.

- there's no other option

🎧 Listen again and repeat.

4. Practice the conversation with a partner.

Pronunciation **F**ocus: Stress

🎧 **5.** Listen and repeat.

    a. That's easier said than done.

    b. They have to have the right skills.

    c. I'd rather not do that.

    d. We don't have a choice.

BUSINESS CONNECTIONS

LISTENING

What else can we offer?

1. Ron Galliano is the benefits coordinator at an international company. He is on a video-conference call with Dorothy Adams and Robert Tanaka. Listen and circle the correct answers.

   a. Dorothy is having problems _____ employees.
   1. attracting   2. keeping
   b. Robert is having problems _____ employees.
   1. attracting   2. keeping
   c. Dorothy would like to offer _____.
   1. executive "perks"   2. flextime
   d. Robert would like to offer _____.
   1. flextime   2. better pay

2. Listen again and check (✓) the five benefits mentioned.

   ___ **a.** health insurance
   ___ **b.** pension plan
   ✓ **c.** company credit card
   ___ **d.** health club membership
   ___ **e.** business class travel
   ___ **f.** end-of-year bonus
   ___ **g.** flextime

NUMBERS

3. Look at the table. Then listen and fill in the missing data.

Average Number of Hours Worked Per Year		
	1980	**1997**
United States	1,883	1,966
Japan	2,121	_____
France	1,880	_____
Germany	1,742	_____
Hong Kong and China	▬	_____
South Korea	▬	_____
Latin America	▬	1,800– _____

Source: The Boston Globe

Listen again and check your answers.

SPEAKING

Which benefits are important to you?

4. Look at the benefits chart below. Check (✓) which benefits are necessary, which ones are desirable, and which ones are not necessary in your industry.

Work with a partner and discuss your answers.

Example

A: I think health insurance is necessary. You need to have that.
B: I agree. And you have to offer a company credit card.
A: Why do you say that? I don't think . . .

Benefits	Necessary	Desirable	Not necessary
health insurance			
company credit card			
company pension plan			
health club membership			
vacation (how much?)			
business class travel			
yearly cash bonuses			
flextime			
pager/cell phone/laptop computer			
other:			

5. Look at the chart again and discuss which benefits are the most important to you.

Conversation Strategies

Asking for an Explanation
- Why do you say that?
- Could you explain that?
- I don't quite see what you mean.

Go to the extra speaking activity on page 96.

READING

The New Leadership

1. Read the article.

Business Culture

In the twenty-first century, managers looking to get ahead will need a completely different set of skills. Technology, products, markets, and customers are changing fast, and corporations will need managers that can handle uncertainty. These leaders will also need the ability to work as part of a team, have concerns for the needs of employees, and also have a sense of humor.

In order to survive, corporations will have to establish an increasing number of partnerships with suppliers, distributors, and their most important customers. Leaders will have to rely more than ever on their staff to act independently to maintain these relationships. As a result, they will also need to build a different kind of relationship with the people who work for them: one based on trust, rather than seniority. The best leaders will favor a team-based approach to management.

In addition, skilled employees will be more in demand, so they will be freer to come and go as they please. Managers will have to make more of an effort to attract new talent and to respond to the needs of their existing employees. Listening skills and a desire to help people could well become important qualities in a successful manager. Also, increased globalization will require sensitivity to other people's traditions and languages.

Source: Business Week

2. Match the beginnings of the sentences with the correct endings to create a summary of the article.

_3_ **a.** Managers will need to be able to handle uncertainty

___ **b.** They will need a different relationship with employees

___ **c.** They will need good listening skills

___ **d.** They will have to be sensitive to other cultures

1. because they will depend on them more.

2. in order to respond to the needs of their staff.

3. because the business world is changing very fast.

4. because more business will be done with international partners.

Talk About It

3. Discuss these questions.

a. Look at the list of qualities in the box. Which three qualities do you think are the most important for managers in your industry?

| a team player | adaptable | loyal | open to new ideas |
| a risk taker | cautious | creative | a sense of humor |

b. Different industries look for different qualities in their managers. How is the approach to management in your business different from other industries?

WRITING

Summary of a Meeting

4. Read the following summary.

To: James Kahn, Grace Matsui, William Owens, Beth Schwab, Evan Torres
From: William Owens
Date: July 19, 2001

Subject: Meeting to discuss recruitment on 7/16

Here is a brief summary of our meeting:
1. Everyone agreed that we need a more aggressive hiring policy. The lack of qualified applicants is a problem in all departments.

2. James suggested recruiting internationally. He pointed out the advantages and disadvantages of this strategy. Beth will consult with the legal department about the issues and procedures involved.

3. Evan suggested offering rewards to employees who help us find new employees. We agreed that this could be a possible strategy. However, we have to work out specific guidelines. Evan agreed to investigate this option.

Read the following notes and write a summary of this meeting.

Useful Language

- Everybody agreed that we need ___.
- There was considerable discussion about ___.
- He pointed out that ___.
- She agreed/ offered to ___.

9/11/01 Meeting about Management Issues
Present: Luis Calvo, Monica Lin, Carlos Moran

1. Agreed: need to reduce amount of overtime worked and rising costs.
2. Carlos: we have to look at recent staff cuts. People are missing deadlines.
3. Monica: absenteeism and lateness are problems in some plants. Monica to review absenteeism/lateness policies with plant managers.
4. Luis to work out realistic targets and propose deadlines to achieve them.

Motivation and Productivity

BUSINESS TALK

GETTING STARTED

1. Some managers are discussing how to motivate employees to
work harder. Read the notes on the flip chart.

> **OUR GOAL**
>
> BETTER MOTIVATION →
> HIGHER PRODUCTIVITY !!
>
> • Employees want to work hard
> • Less turnover: Employees will
> stay with the company
>
> POSSIBLE SOLUTIONS
>
> • Better pay and/or benefits
> • Bonus plan tied to job performance
> • Training to meet employees needs
> • Opportunities for promotion

**What do you think? Combine phrases from each column to
form three sentences.**

If employees (don't) get performance bonuses,		be more productive.
If there aren't opportunities for further training,	they will (they'll)	be more motivated.
		be loyal to the company.
If employees (don't) participate in decision making,	they won't	feel more responsible. (your own idea)

Example

*If employees get performance bonuses, they will be more
productive.*

2. What are some other ways to motivate employees? Discuss
your opinions with a partner.

Example

A: In my opinion, if employees . . .
B: Absolutely . . .

> In my opinion, . . .
> If you ask me, . . .
> Absolutely.
> I'm not sure. I think . . .

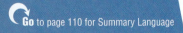

Go to page 110 for Summary Language

CONVERSATION

We'll be in real trouble if we don't do something.

🎧 **3.** Read and listen to the conversation.

Paul thinks we need to reduce the training budget. What do you all think? Susan?

To be honest, I don't like the idea.

Really? Why?

If we cut the budget, we won't be able to provide the most up-to-date technology training.

- How do you all feel about that?   • Frankly

- What don't you like about it?   • keep up with changes in technology

But we'll be in real trouble if we don't do something to reduce costs.

I understand that.

I think we should cut expenses in other areas first—like travel budgets.

I see what you mean. What do the rest of you think?

- find some way   • realize

- In my opinion   • That's a good point.

🎧 Listen again and repeat.

4. Practice the conversation with a partner.

Pronunciation Focus: Stress

🎧 **5.** Listen and repeat.

    a. I understand that.

    b. I realize that.

    c. I see what you mean.

    d. That's a good point.

LISTENING

Here's the problem.

1. A team of sales managers is having a meeting. Listen and circle the correct answers.

  a. What problem are the managers discussing?
  1. training
  2. falling sales
  3. productivity

  b. What is the main reason for the problem?
  1. low motivation
  2. competition
  3. turnover

  c. How do the managers propose to solve the problem?
  1. offer more benefits
  2. lower sales quotas for bonuses
  3. hire more salespeople

2. Listen. Complete the notes.

Average sales per person per quarter:	_____
Current quota:	_____
Proposed new quota:	_____

3. Complete the sentence.

Mike believes that if they lower the quotas, _____
_____.

NUMBERS

4. Listen to another discussion at the same meeting. Fill in the table.

	Percentage change	Dollars	Yen
United States	+9.8%		
Asia			
Europe			
Latin America			

Listen again and check your answers.

SPEAKING

If we want to increase productivity,...

5. Work with a partner. You are consultants to a large telecommunications company. The company faces competition from large international corporations and has a number of other problems.

Read the fact sheet.

Conversation Strategies

Agreeing with Reservations

- I see what you mean. But if we do that, ___.
- That's a good point. But it doesn't solve the problem of ___.
- I agree. But we also need to consider ___.

F A C T   S H E E T

- Productivity is 37 percent lower than in similar companies overseas.
- Customers are frequently without services.
- Employees are poorly trained at all levels.
- Little attention is paid to the quality of customer service.

Choose two of the problems and discuss ways to solve them. Use some of the ideas in the box as well as your own.

> training   bonuses tied to job performance
> hiring guidelines   new equipment and systems

Example

A: *Let's discuss what to do about productivity.*
B: *In my opinion, the company will need to invest in training, if it wants to increase productivity. I think…*

Go to the extra speaking activity on page 97.

READING

Making Meetings More Productive

1. Read the article.

Business Culture

Many managers and workers complain about unproductive meetings. White-collar workers spend on average one to one and a half days each week in meetings, according to a survey last year by 3M Meeting Network, an online resource for running effective meetings. Managers spend as much as 33 hours a week in conferences. And meetings are increasing as more employees work in teams.

How do you ensure that your meetings are productive? First, decide whether a meeting is really necessary. If you just need to give information to workers, it's better to use e-mail or a memo. It's also a lot cheaper than pulling employees away from work. Second, invite only those who really need to attend.

Third, send out the agenda and reading materials before the meeting so that people attending can do their homework. Lack of preparation is one of the top complaints about meetings, according to the 3M survey.

The most productive meetings are those done in small groups of four or five. Small meetings tend to be more focused than large ones. They also force participants to be prepared. You can't hide in a small meeting.

Start the meeting on time, and don't let it run on too long. One way to do this is to schedule it just before the end of the workday. And if people still want to sit and chat for too long, some experts have a dramatic solution: Take away the chairs and hold short meetings standing up!

Source: Lexis-Nexis; The Indianapolis Star

2. Write *T* (true) or *F* (false) according to the article.

_F_ **a.** Managers spend on average one to one and a half days each week in meetings.

___ **b.** Workers have more meetings nowadays.

___ **c.** Some meetings are not necessary.

___ **d.** It's important to give participants an agenda when they arrive at a meeting.

___ **e.** Small meetings are less productive.

Talk About It

3. Discuss the following questions.

a. Which two of the following are most important for a successful meeting? Why?

> a written agenda   a clear objective   a time limit
> preparation before the meeting   visual aids

b. Which advice in the list below would NOT be appropriate in your business culture or in your country?

- Use e-mail for discussion instead of holding a meeting.
- Invite only the people who really need to attend.
- Start the meeting on time, even if some people haven't arrived.

WRITING

Writing an Agenda

4. Look at the following agenda for a meeting.

General Products, Inc.

Meeting Time: November 2, 10:00–11:00
Location: Conference Room
Attendees: Meg Stanley, Anna Kwo, Jim Matsumoto, Rob Samuels
Objective: Decision on new incentive/bonus plan

AGENDA

1. Present results of staff satisfaction questionnaire   (MS)
2. Review bonus plans of competitors   (JM)
3. Present cost estimates of different plans   (RS)
4. Brainstorm: discuss other possible solutions   (all)
5. Make decision   (all)
6. Other business

Useful Language

- present results/ estimates
- review ___ plans
- brainstorm possible solutions
- make a decision

5. Read the notes below and complete the agenda for a meeting. Put the items in a logical order. (More than one order is possible.)

General Products, Inc.

Meeting Time: March 5, 11:00–12:00
Location: Meeting Room
Attendees: Tom Zinner, Barbara Ma, Steven Sumiya, Shelly Camargo
Objective: _____

AGENDA

1.   _Present latest sales figures (SS)._
   _____
   _____
   _____
   _____
   _____
   _____
   _____

Discuss latest sales figures and delivery problem

Tom: report on competitor's delivery system.

Steve: Present latest sales figures

Shelly: present consultant's report on our current delivery system.

Other business: Barbara to present a few different logo designs: pick new logo; anything else?

Brainstorm solutions to delivery problem.

Advertising Strategies

GETTING STARTED

1. Three executives are discussing an advertising campaign for a new line of stereo equipment. Listen and check (✓) the types of advertising that they mention.

- ☐ radio advertising
- ☐ magazine advertising
- ☐ TV commercials
- ☐ billboards
- ☐ the Web
- ☐ direct mail

OBJECTIVES

- To suggest advertising strategies

- To propose a website design

- To respond to a marketing survey

2. Listen again and circle the correct choice.

a. What approaches *can/could* we use to appeal to that market?

b. If we bought TV airtime, we *will/would* be well over budget.

c. Radio advertising *might/will* work, if we placed the ads well.

d. What if we *advertise/advertised* on billboards?

e. I think billboards could work, if we *focus/focused* on subway and train advertising.

3. Work with a partner. Look at the box in exercise 1 and discuss how you would advertise the stereo equipment or one of the following: a new credit card, a new soft drink, ready-to-eat dinners.

Example

A: What if we advertised the stereo equipment in magazines?
B: That's a good idea. I would also place ads on the Web.

 Go to page 111 for Summary Language

CONVERSATION

Maybe we could go for both.

🎧 **4.** Read and listen to the conversation.

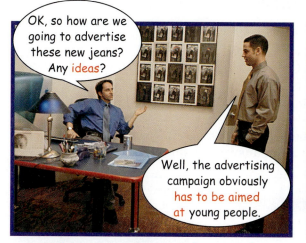

OK, so how are we going to advertise these new jeans? Any ideas?

Well, the advertising campaign obviously has to be aimed at young people.

• suggestions   • needs to appeal to

It would be nice if we could do something dramatic . . .

What if we advertised on rock radio stations?

• Could we advertise

Yes, and it wouldn't be too expensive.

That would reach the right audience.

• have an immediate effect

If I were you, I'd look at websites for teenagers.

Well, maybe we could go for both.

• I think you should   • consider

🎧 Listen again and repeat.

5. Practice the conversation with a partner.

Pronunciation Focus: Stress with *would* and *could*

🎧 **6.** Listen and repeat.

    a. It would be nice if we could do something dramatic.

    b. That would reach the right audience.

    c. It wouldn't be too expensive.

    d. Maybe we could go for both.

BUSINESS CONNECTIONS

LISTENING

What kind of image do you want to project?

🎧 **1.** A web design consultant is giving advice to business owners about creating a website. Listen and then circle the answer.

Her main point is that a company home page should:
a. be visually appealing, with a variety of colors and boxes.
b. present as much information as possible so that people don't have to use links.
c. have clear information, but be simple and not too long.

🎧 **2.** Look at the home page she discusses. Read the questions. Then listen again and answer the questions.

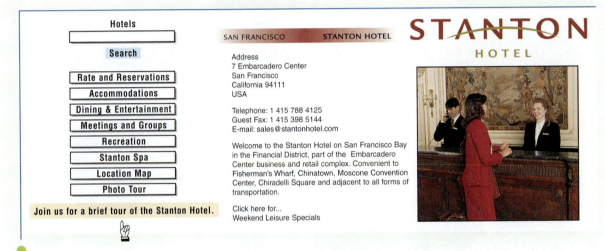

a. What three rules does the consultant give for good website design?

_____

_____

_____

b. What criticism does the consultant have of the Stanton Hotel's home page?

_____

NUMBERS

🎧 **3.** Listen and fill in the table.

	2000	2002	2005
Internet Users (Worldwide)	259M		
US Percentage			

🎧 Listen again and check your answers.

SPEAKING

Ideas for a Home Page

4. Work with a partner. Look at the photographs of the Executive Hotel. Discuss which photo(s) would be the best to use on a website home page for the hotel.

Example

A: What if we included the photo of the lobby?
B: Yes, but . . .

Conversation Strategies

Moving a Discussion Forward
- We need to move on.
- We don't have much time left. Let's discuss ___.
- OK. Are we ready to decide?

5. Look at the notes below. Discuss which information should be included on the home page and which links to provide. Draw a simple picture, using the home page on page 82 as a guide.

Example

A: It would be nice if we could include information about the fitness center.
B: Yes, but maybe we should make this a link so we can have a few photos on it.

Executive Hotel—website ideas
Image: very comfortable, luxurious; good facilities for business travelers.
(use 1 or 2 photos on home page)

Address, telephone, and fax number of hotel must be on home page.

Emphasize the business center, meeting facilities, and central location.

Other facilities: restaurants, karaoke bar, fitness center & spa, 24-hour room service.

All rooms with city view.
Include info. about the area and directions from airport. Include registration form.
Other?

Go to the extra speaking activity on page 97.

READING

Marketing Across Cultures

1. Read the article.

Business Culture

The story is often told about General Motors trying to sell their Nova model car in Latin America and finding out that "no va" literally means "it doesn't go" in Spanish.

But cultural awareness in marketing is a lot more than careful translation. There are many more subtle differences between cultures. For example, colors that seem attractive in one culture may be unattractive or tasteless in another. Schedules, transportation, and everyday routines differ widely. And the simplest cultural differences can upset the greatest plans.

In Japan, for example, a US household products company spent millions of dollars on a marketing campaign to introduce its laundry detergent. Nevertheless, sales were very low. In fact, few stores even stocked the soap. The reason? The typically American "large, economy-sized" boxes were far too big for the Japanese market. The product required too much space to stock and the boxes were very heavy to carry.

In Europe and in much of Asia, product comparisons in advertising are not accepted or allowed. Declaring that one soft drink tastes better than another, or that one automobile is more dependable than another, could be met with distaste or even legal action. Many cultures prefer a more humble approach and consider American advertising too loud and aggressive. US companies doing business overseas may find that an approach that emphasizes company longevity and reputation may work better.

Source: Lexis-Nexis; World Trade Magazine

2. Check (✓) which of the following topics are mentioned in the article.

✓ **a.** Translation of product names
___ **b.** Religious beliefs and superstitions
___ **c.** Different preferences for colors
___ **d.** Animals and cartoon characters used in advertising
___ **e.** Differences in national and regional cuisine
___ **f.** Differences in living styles and habits
___ **g.** Differences in marketing and advertising styles

Talk About It

3. Look at the list above. Describe the marketing mistakes that an overseas company might make when advertising a product in your country. As an alternative, describe a marketing campaign that has failed due to cultural differences.

WRITING

Responding to a Survey

4. A US manager is responding to a marketing survey from the company's head office overseas. Read the e-mail. His responses are in blue type.

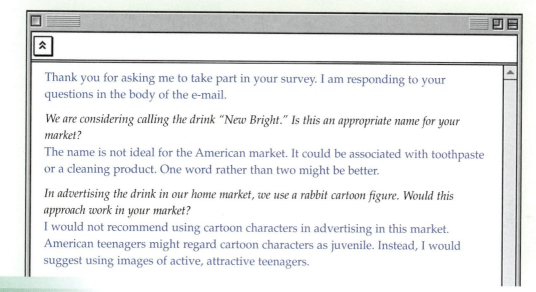

Thank you for asking me to take part in your survey. I am responding to your questions in the body of the e-mail.

We are considering calling the drink "New Bright." Is this an appropriate name for your market?
The name is not ideal for the American market. It could be associated with toothpaste or a cleaning product. One word rather than two might be better.

In advertising the drink in our home market, we use a rabbit cartoon figure. Would this approach work in your market?
I would not recommend using cartoon characters in advertising in this market. American teenagers might regard cartoon characters as juvenile. Instead, I would suggest using images of active, attractive teenagers.

Useful Language

- I would not recommend ___.
- ___ would be more suitable for our market.
- I would suggest ___.

5. You have received the following request from your head office in the US. Choose two questions to answer. Write your response.

```
We would like to introduce our brand of ready-to-eat soups to your
market. These soups are made with the freshest ingredients and come
in three flavors: tomato, mushroom, and corn. They are sold in the
refrigerated section of supermarkets in cartons that contain enough
soup for a single serving. They are popular with busy professionals
who have limited time to cook.

To determine if this product is appropriate for other markets, we
are sending this survey to all of our overseas managers. We would
be grateful if you could take a few minutes to answer the following
questions.

1. Would this product appeal to consumers in your market? If so,
   which consumers would be most likely to buy this product?
2. Which of the flavors would be most popular in your market? The
   least popular? Are there any other flavors we should consider?
3. Is the single-serving carton size appropriate for your market?
   Why or why not?
4. What would be the most effective way to advertise?

Thank you for your time.
```

SPEAKING

What type of company is NTT?

4. Speaker B, look at the chart below and answer Speaker A's questions.

Example

Speaker A: *What type of company is NTT Communications?*
Speaker B: *It's a telecommunications company.*

NTT Communications
Type of company: Telecommunications
Head office: _____
Employees: 6,700 worldwide
Current activities: _____

Hanjin Shipping
Type of company: _____
Head office: Seoul, Korea
Employees: _____
Current activities: Expanding service to China

Unibanco
Type of company: Banking and finance
Head Office: _____
Employees: 19,500
Current activities: _____

5. Now ask Speaker A for the information you need and complete the chart. Use the questions in the box below.

Conversation Strategies

Clarifying information
- Could you repeat that?
- Excuse me?
- How do you spell that?

What type of company is _____?	Where is the head office of _____?
How many employees does it have?	What is the company doing now?

6. What do you know about these companies? Talk about the ones that you know. Use the phrases in the box.

It sells/manufactures/provides . . .
It's based in . . .
Right now, it's . . .

Go to the extra speaking activity on page 93.

ACTIVITY FILE

When are you available?

4. Speaker B, your client, Speaker A, will be in your city next week. Look at your schedule and arrange a time to meet. Use the phrases in the box. Write the appointment in your schedule.

> I'm available after . . .
> I'm afraid I can't make it . . .
> I'm sorry, I'm busy . . .
> So, when can you make it?
> How about . . . ?

Example

A: *I'm coming to (your city) next week for a few days. Could we set up a meeting?*

B: *Of course. When are you available?*

MONDAY

June 13th	Morning:	Flight leaves 8:40 a.m. for Garden City Conference
	Afternoon:	
	Evening:	Returning 7:05 p.m.

TUESDAY

June 14th	Morning:	9:00 Sales meeting
	Afternoon:	
	Evening:	8:00 Dinner, Pepino's Restaurant

WEDNESDAY

June 15th	Morning:	11:00 interview, Brian de Soto
	Afternoon:	1:00 lunch, Barbara Scott
	Evening:	

THURSDAY

June 16th	Morning:	
	Afternoon:	3:00 George Lee
	Evening:	

---

5. Look at your own schedule for next week. Make arrangements with Speaker A for the following:

- a meeting in the morning
- a visit to a company in the afternoon
- dinner one evening

Conversation Strategies

Accepting an Invitation

- I'd like to (have dinner).
- That would be very nice. Thank you.
- That would be great.

Go to the extra speaking activity on page 93.

SPEAKING

How long has he had this job?

3. You and Speaker A are colleagues at Northwest Bank. You want to hire an executive assistant and are considering two candidates.

   Speaker B, ask Speaker A about Cristina Lee. Use the questions in the box as well as your own. Complete the chart.

   > What is she doing now?   Where did she . . . ?
   > How long has she had this job? Does she have . . . ?

   ### Example

   B: What is Christina doing now?
   A: She's an executive assistant at the Santa Clara branch.

Name:	Cristina Lee
Current position:	Executive Assistant, Northwest Bank, Santa Clara branch
How long in this position:	
Previous experience:	
Computer skills:	
Education:	
Other information:	Cristina's boss recommends her highly, but some coworkers find her hard to work with.

4. Read about Paul Martin and answer Speaker A's questions.

Name:	Paul Martin
Current position:	Administrative Assistant, Sales Dept., PY Finance Company
How long in this position:	2 years part-time; 6 months full-time
Previous experience:	(student)
Computer skills:	excellent
Education:	BA in Business, just graduated
Other information:	Paul's father is a good friend of the bank president. He will work hard.

Conversation Strategies

Disagreeing Politely
- I'm not sure I agree.
- Do you think so?
- Yes, but don't you think _____?

5. Talk about the candidates. Look at all the information. Who do you want to hire? Give two reasons.

Go to the extra speaking activity on page 94.

ACTIVITY FILE

UNIT 5, PAGE 29

SPEAKING

Sales reached a peak.

Conversation Strategies

Controlling the Flow of Information

- Just a minute.
- Can we back up a minute?
- Let me get that down.

4. Speaker B, listen to Speaker A and complete the graph below.

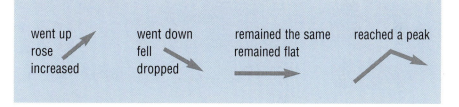

450XG Sales 1996 – 2002

16,000
15,000
14,000
1996 1997 1998 1999 2000 2001 2002

5. Use the words in the box and describe the sales graph of the 350LG truck below to Speaker A.

went up	went down	remained the same	reached a peak
rose	fell	remained flat	
increased	dropped		

Example

In 1996, sales went up to 15,500.
Then the figures went up/down to . . .

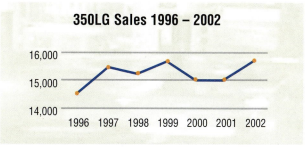

350LG Sales 1996 – 2002

16,000
15,000
14,000
1996 1997 1998 1999 2000 2001 2002

6. Give reasons for the rising or falling sales on the graph in exercise 5. Use some of the reasons in the box or your own ideas.

> We ran an advertising campaign.
> We changed the price.
> We faced increasing competition.
> The customers didn't like the design.

Go to the extra speaking activity on page 94.

SPEAKING

Two Ways to Buy Groceries

4. Speaker B, listen to Speaker A's description of the traditional process. Complete the sentences in the flow chart below.

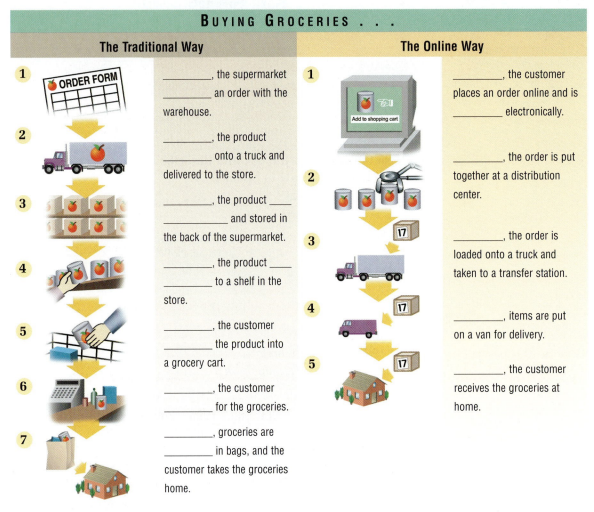

BUYING GROCERIES . . .

The Traditional Way	The Online Way

The Traditional Way

1. _____, the supermarket _____ an order with the warehouse.

2. _____, the product _____ onto a truck and delivered to the store.

3. _____, the product _____ _____ and stored in the back of the supermarket.

4. _____, the product _____ _____ to a shelf in the store.

5. _____, the customer _____ the product into a grocery cart.

6. _____, the customer _____ for the groceries.

7. _____, groceries are _____ in bags, and the customer takes the groceries home.

The Online Way

1. _____, the customer places an order online and is _____ electronically.

2. _____, the order is put together at a distribution center.

3. _____, the order is loaded onto a truck and taken to a transfer station.

4. _____, items are put on a van for delivery.

5. _____, the customer receives the groceries at home.

5. Look at the steps involved in online buying in the chart above. Use the words in the box and describe the process to Speaker A.

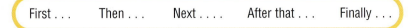

First . . .   Then . . .   Next . . . .   After that . . .   Finally . . .

Conversation Strategies

Checking for Understanding

■ Do you want me to repeat that?

■ Do you have any questions?

■ Is that clear?

Example

B: First, the customer places an order online and is billed electronically.

6. Discuss the two processes. Which steps are eliminated or changed when customers buy online?

Go to the extra speaking activity on page 94.

SPEAKING

I'm calling about the pagers.

3. Speaker B, read Situation 1 and follow the instructions.

SITUATION 1

Speaker B, you are the sales manager of a telephone pager company. Your new pager has been very popular with your customers. Unfortunately, some parts needed for manufacturing were held up because of a strike. Most orders are several weeks behind schedule.

Speaker A, an important client, is calling you. The client ordered 40 pagers one month ago. His order is due to be shipped next week.

Think about what you are going to say. Then, take the call. Do what you can to keep the client happy.

Example

A: *I'm calling about our order. We haven't received the pagers.*
B: *I'm sorry for the delay. Unfortunately,….*

Conversation Strategies

Ending a Conversation by Promising Action

- ▪ OK. I'll tell you what. I'll _____.
- ▪ Anyway, why don't I _____?
- ▪ All right. Let me discuss this with _____, and I'll get back to you.

4. Read Situation 2 and follow the instructions.

SITUATION 2

You are the senior manager of a large company. A team of computer specialists is installing a new software system in your workplace. This project is important and expensive. The team has been at your office for about a month. You are worried about how much longer the project will take. You have not received a progress report.

Speaker A is the project manager. Tell him or her that you are concerned about how long the project is taking.

Example

B: *How's the software project going? We need to know how much longer it will take.*
A: *The project is going well…*

Go to the extra speaking activity on page 95.

ACTIVITY FILE

SPEAKING

How do they compare?

5. Speaker B, look at the information about the PQ 5 and answer Speaker A's questions.

Conversation Strategies

Correcting Information

- ■ Actually, it's not fifty-three. It's sixty-three.
- ■ Sorry. I meant to say three hours, not six.
- ■ No, there is an internal modem.

Example

A: *How much does the PQ 5 cost?*
B: *It's $2,163 dollars.*

Model	PQ 5	NS 3
Price	$2,163	*$1,521*
Memory (RAM)	64 MB	
Screen Size	14.1 in	
Internal Modem	yes	
Battery Life	6 hr	
Weight	4.3 lb	
Technical Support	Lifetime phone and internet support	

6. Ask Speaker A for information about the NS 3 and fill in the chart. Use the words in the box.

> How much . . . ?   How big . . . ?   How long . . . ?   Is there . . . ?

7. Compare the two laptops. What are the main differences? Which do you prefer? Use the words in the box and your own ideas.

> It's faster/smaller/cheaper/more useful than . . .
> It has more power/memory/features than . . .

Go to the extra speaking activity on page 96.

EXTRA SPEAKING ACTIVITIES

UNIT 1
TALKING ABOUT YOUR COMPANY

Work with a partner. Name a company in your city or area for each industry. Share information to fill in the chart.

Industry	Name of company	Head office	What does it do?	Other information
Manufacturing				
Transportation				
Telecommunications				
Banking				
Software				
Insurance				

UNIT 2
MAKING CONVERSATION

Work with a partner. Role-play the following situation:

Speaker A, Speaker B is visiting your company. This is his or her first visit to your city. Think of three interesting places that you want Speaker B to see. You have met Speaker B at the airport, and you are riding in a taxi to his or her hotel. Make small talk. Ask about the flight and tell Speaker B about the three places.

Speaker B, you have just arrived in Speaker A's city. You are riding together in a taxi from the airport to your hotel. You have never been to this city before. Make small talk with Speaker A and respond to his or her suggestions.

Then switch roles.

UNIT 3
ARRANGING MEETINGS AND SCHEDULES

1. Write down the days of the workweek (Monday-Friday) and fill in the calendar with your evening activities for this week. If you are free every evening, select one or two activities from the box to write in your calendar.

> **EVENING ACTIVITIES**
>
> tennis game with a friend
> an evening class
> plans for dinner with. . .
> preparing for a meeting the next day
> exercising at gym

2. Work with a partner. Look at your calendar. Have a conversation to arrange a time to have dinner together at a restaurant this week. Decide on a day, a time, and a place.

EXTRA SPEAKING ACTIVITIES

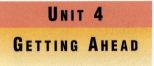

UNIT 4
GETTING AHEAD

1. Fill in information about yourself in one of the lists below.

If you are employed:

Current position: _____

How long in this position: _____

Previous experience: _____

_____

Computer skills: _____

Education: _____

Other information: _____

_____

If you are a student:

Current year in school: _____

Expected graduation date: _____

Area of study (major): _____

_____

Computer skills: _____

Work experience: _____

Other information: _____

_____

2. Work with a partner. Take turns interviewing each other about what you have been doing the past several years.

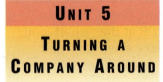

UNIT 5
TURNING A COMPANY AROUND

1. Work with a partner. Look at the sales performance for two competing motorcycle models, the Ace 900 and the Shark 77.

Speaker A, prepare a brief presentation about the performance of the Ace 900. Speaker B, prepare a brief presentation about the Shark 77. Describe the changes in sales and give reasons.

Motorcycle Sales: 1997-2001

	1997	1998	1999	2000	2001
Ace 900	11,900	13,200	14,000	14,500	13,000
Shark 77	9,000	10,300	13,100	13,700	14,000

2. Speaker A, give your presentation to Speaker B, and answer any questions.

Speaker B, listen to Speaker A's presentation and ask questions.

3. Speaker B, give your presentation to Speaker A and answer any questions.

UNIT 6
DESCRIBING A PROCESS

Work with a partner. Role-play the following situation:

Speaker A, describe the steps in the hiring process at your company or a company you know about to Speaker B, who is interested in applying for a job.

Speaker B, listen to Speaker A's description and ask questions.

Then switch roles.

EXTRA SPEAKING ACTIVITIES

UNIT 7
TEAMWORK

1. Look at the list of things to do for a presentation next week. Decide which tasks you want to do.

- Reserve a room for the presentation.

- Make sure the audio-visual equipment (VCR, overhead projector) is working properly the day before.

- Write up and prepare several visuals or handouts to go with your presentation.

- Meet guests.

- Write up notes for introducing two special guests. Be responsible for introducing them at the presentation.

- Organize the room and the refreshments (coffee, tea, mineral water, etc.).

2. Work with a partner. Discuss what has to be done for the presentation. Suggest tasks your partner could do, and say what you would like to do. At least once, say you would rather not do one of the tasks.

UNIT 8
MANAGING CHANGE

1. What recent company changes do you know about? See how many different companies you can think of and write them down.

Think of a company that has:

appointed a new CEO	_____
hired many new employees	_____
laid off employees	_____
opened a new store	_____
moved into a new building	_____
earned good profits	_____
had falling sales figures	_____
restructured a division	_____

2. Work with a partner and discuss these changes.

UNIT 9
CLIENTS AND CUSTOMERS

Work with a partner. Role-play the following situation:

Speaker A, you work for a company that is giving an important sales presentation at a conference tomorrow. You requested a room for 300 people, but the conference organizers gave you a room that is much too small. It only fits 150 people. Call the organizers. Explain the problem and ask for a larger room.

Speaker B, you are one of the conference organizers. Take the call from Speaker A. Apologize for the error. A larger room is not available at the conference hotel. Offer to find another meeting space at a nearby hotel.

Then switch roles.

UNIT 10
CORPORATE GOALS

1. What are your plans and expectations for the next year, either for work or for school? What will you probably do? What do you hope to do? Make a short list.

2. Work with a partner. Have a conversation about your plans. Use the words in the box. Then listen to each other's plans and ask questions.

plan to	hope to	expect to
might	will probably	aim to

UNIT 11
DESCRIBING AND COMPARING PRODUCTS

Work with a partner. You are both interested in buying a new wireless phone. Look at the information in the box. Discuss which model you would prefer to buy and explain why.

	Model X	Model Y
Price	$150.00	$145.00
Dimensions	4.5 by 2 in	3.7 by 2 in
Weight	5.5 oz	4.2 oz
Battery Life	2.5 hr	4.2 hr

UNIT 12
CHALLENGES TO MANAGEMENT

1. Look at this list of benefits and opportunities at a company. Rank the benefits from 1-6, with 1 as the benefit most important to you.

_____ flextime

_____ more vacation days

_____ opportunity to telecommute or work from home

_____ opportunity to take courses that will help you advance at your company

_____ health club at your company

_____ variety of social activities offered by company (sports, entertainment, etc.)

2. Work with a partner. Explain your choices. Say why each benefit is or is not important to you. Then compare your lists. How do they differ?

EXTRA SPEAKING ACTIVITIES

Read the memo below and discuss the problems with a partner. Talk about possible solutions and give your opinion.

MEMO

TO: Department Managers
RE: Problems with overseas relocations

As you know, we often send employees overseas to work in our branch offices. Employees are usually asked to move to a country for one to five years. Tomorrow we will be discussing the following problems and talking about solutions.

1. More experienced managers usually have families that relocate with them. Families often face problems with the language and culture, and with education for their children.
2. Overseas employees are asking for an increased travel budget so they can come home more than once a year.
3. Younger employees have fewer problems adjusting in a foreign country, but often lack the business experience needed in the branch offices.
4. Younger employees are often less loyal to the company, and sometimes leave for a job with a competitor.

Work with a partner. Develop an advertising strategy for the product described in the box below. Discuss the following questions:

1. What is the market for this product? Describe the typical customer in terms of age and income (high, average, low).
2. Which types of advertising would be the most effective? Choose two from this list: Radio, magazine, TV, billboard, the Web, direct mail. Explain why they would be the best choices for the product.
3. Describe a possible advertisement. How would it look? What would it say?

Handheld Computer/Organizer (PDA)

Expandable organizer, turns into a digital camera, music player or phone
8MG RAM Stores 12,000 addresses, 10 years of appointments, 6,000 to-do items.
Comes in 6 colors.
$260.00

Nouns

annual income	executive
client	head office
corporation	headset
dress code	suit
employee	supplier

Industries

banking
consulting services
finance/financial services
Internet services
shipping
telecommunications
transportation

Adjectives and Adverbs

casual (adj.)
formal/informal (adj.)
worldwide (adv.)

Verbs

design	manufacture
develop	market
employ	provide
expand	sell
hire	supply

Expressions

Are you based in ___?
Oh.
Really?
That's interesting.
What does your company do?

Conversation Strategies:
Clarifying Information

Could you repeat that?
Excuse me?
How do you spell that?

Useful Language

We are recognized as a world leader in _____.
Enclosed is a catalogue that describes _____.
Please feel free to call me for further
 information.

Simple Present

Affirmative Statements

I	**work**	We	
You	**work**	You	**work**
He/She/It	**works**	They	

Negative Statements

I	**don't**	
He/She/It	**doesn't**	**work**

We			
You	**don't**	**work**
They		

Present Continuous

Affirmative and Negative Statements

I	**am**	
You	**are**	(not) **working**
He/She/It	**is**	

We	**are**	(not) **working**
They		

• Use the **simple present** to describe
  something that is always true or true in
  general.

  *Plantronics Inc. **designs** and **manufactures**
  lightweight headsets.*

• Use the **present continuous** to describe
  something that is true at the moment
  or for a limited time.

  *Plantronics **is** currently **marketing** its
  products for home use.*

Nouns

paperwork
software engineer
training

Socializing

bill	meal
business lunch	menu
city	mineral water
coffee	small talk
fan (sports)	soccer
food	sports
guest	tea
host	trip

Adjectives

delicious	nice
excellent	popular
exciting	wonderful

Verbs

enjoy   order   like

Expressions

Actually . . .
Can I get you something to drink?
Could I get you a cup of coffee?
Did you have a good trip?
How's it going?
No, thanks.
Right.
That's right.
Would you like some help with the menu?

Wh- questions

What do you recommend?
What do you think of ___?
What part of ___ are you from?
What would you like to drink?

Conversation Strategies:

Making Small Talk

You're from ___, aren't you?
Is this your first visit to ___?
Do you like ___?
You enjoy ___, don't you?
Tell me, do you follow ___? (a sport)
What about you?

Useful Language

I appreciated your feedback about ___.
As I mentioned during lunch, ___.

Tag Questions

A **tag question** is a question added at the end of a sentence. If the statement is affirmative, the tag is usually negative. If the statement is negative, the tag is usually affirmative.

Affirmative Statement + Negative Tag

---

*It's a wonderful city, **isn't it**?*
*That **was** a wonderful meal, **wasn't it**?*
*You live in Sao Paulo, **don't you**?*

Negative Statement + Affirmative Tag

---

*You **aren't** in the computer industry, **are you**?*
*You **don't** follow soccer much, **do you**?*

- Use a tag question to check that something is true.

  *You're in the computer industry, **aren't you**?*

- Use a tag question when you think the other person will agree.

  *It's a wonderful city, **isn't it**?*

Nouns

calendar
commute
gesture
manufacturing plant
rush hour
schedule
sightseeing
system
videoconferencing

Events

meeting (planning, sales)
presentation (design, sales)
appointment
flight
trade show

Verbs

arrange
arrive
schedule

Expressions

Are you available the next day?
Could we set up a meeting?
How about the 25th?
. . . if it's convenient for you.
. . . if it's OK with you.
I'm afraid I can't make it.
I'm sorry, I'm busy on ___.
I'm free after ___.
That sounds good.
That's OK with me.
When can you make it?

Conversation Strategies:
Accepting an Invitation

I'd like to (have dinner).
That would be very nice. Thank you.
That would be great.

Useful Language

If possible, I would like to ___.
Could you please suggest ___?
I'm afraid I won't be available ___.

The Simple Present and Present Continuous for the Future

- Use the **simple present** for scheduled future events. Use the **present continuous** to refer to future plans.

Simple Present for the Future

The plane **leaves** at noon.

Present Continuous for the Future

I'm coming to Sydney next month.

Prepositions of Time: *At, In, On*

- Use *at* with time expressions.

  at nine o'clock, *at* ten-fifteen, *at* noon

- Use *in* with *the morning, the afternoon, the evening.*

  in the morning

- Use *on* with a day or a date.

  on Monday, *on* the 20th, *on* my birthday

Nouns

candidate	marketing
colleague	position
computer skills	product development
degree	promotion
experience	recommendation
fast track	research and
management	development (R&D)

Job Titles

accountant
assistant (executive, administrative)
CEO (Chief Executive Officer)
chairwoman
director
president
sales representative (rep)
vice president

Adjectives

current   senior   previous

Verbs

graduate   recommend   promote

Expressions

I'm delighted to hear that.
I'm with (name of company).
I've wanted to meet you for a long time.
That's excellent news.
What area are you in?

Conversation Strategies:

Disagreeing Politely

I'm not sure I agree.
Do you think so?
Yes, but don't you think ___?

Useful Language

He/She has been with the company for ___ years.
He/She first worked in ___.
He/She took over as ___.
For the past ___ years, he/she has worked in ___.

Present Perfect Tense

Regular verbs and the verb *be*

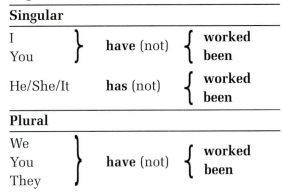

Singular

I You }	**have** (not) {	worked been
He/She/It	**has** (not) {	worked been

Plural

We You They }	**have** (not) {	worked been

- Use the **present perfect** to talk about actions and situations that began in the past and continue in the present.

  *Fiorina **has been** at Hewlett-Packard since 1997.*

Prepositions of Time: *For* and *Since*; *How long . . .?*

- Use *for* to describe a period of time.

  *Fiorina has held senior management positions **for** 20 years.*

- Use *since* to describe a point in time.

  *She has been at Hewlett-Packard **since** 1997.*

- *How long* is often used with the present perfect.

  ***How long have you been** in this position?*

Nouns

competition	market share
competitor	model
customer satisfaction	morale
goal	peak
image	route
keyboard	sales
laptop	sales performance
logo	strategy
market	survey

Adjectives

falling	increasing
flat	(un)profitable

Adverbs

dramatically	steadily
immediately	

Verbs

invest	reduce
redesign	understand

Verbs to Describe Performance

fall	drop
improve	reach (a peak)
increase	remain (flat)
rise	

Expressions

Did you figure it out?
It didn't perform well.
So, what did you do?
We couldn't understand it.

Past Time Expressions

a few years ago
in the early/mid/late 90's
last year

Conversation Strategies:
Controlling the Flow of Information

Just a minute.
Can we back up a minute?
Let me get that down.

Useful Language

We required flight attendants to ___.
We installed/redesigned ___.
We assigned more personnel to ___.
As a result, ___.

Simple Past

Affirmative Statements

Regular Verbs

save	They **saved** the industry.
launch	They **launched** the Swatch brand.

Irregular Verbs

be	The strategy **was** a success.
fall	Sales **fell** in 1983.
go	A sales team **went** to America.

Negative Statements

be	The strategy **wasn't** a success.
fall	Sales **didn't fall** in 2000.
go	A sales team **didn't go** to America.

Questions

be	**Was** it a success?
do	What **did** you **do**?

Past Forms of Other Irregular Verbs

find	**found**	*make*	**made**
have	**had**	*rise*	**rose**
know	**knew**	*sell*	**sold**
lose	**lost**		

Nouns

e-commerce	production
delivery process	résumé
hiring process	status
online	system
performance	team
position	training
process	Web

Shipping and Delivery

cart	shelf
conveyor belt	shipment
delivery	supplier
distribution center	warehouse
package	

Adjectives

interesting	two-step	top

Verbs

advertise	review
deliver	select
evaluate	ship
interview	sort
place	store
rank	unload
remove	

Sequencers

First . . .	After that . . .	Finally . . .
Then . . .	Next . . .	

Expressions

Here's how it works.
How does your management training
   system work?
How's that done?
I see.
Let me explain.
That's an interesting system/process.

Conversation Strategies:
Checking for Understanding

Do you want me to repeat that?
Do you have any questions?
Is that clear?

Useful Language

The items are back ordered/out of
   stock/ready for shipment.
The order was shipped this
   morning/incorrectly addressed/refused
   by customs.

The Passive Voice: Simple Present and Simple Past

Simple Present

The fruit	**is washed**.	
The employees	**are ranked**.	
The evaluations	**are done**	every year.
The packages	**are put**	on a truck.

Simple Past

The order	**was shipped**	last Tuesday.
The items	**were delivered**	this morning.
The box	**was taken**	off the shelf.

- Use the **passive voice** to describe processes and procedures when the focus is on the action that is done rather than on the person who does the action.

Nouns

Trade Fairs and Conventions
accommodation
booth
brochure
conference center
product demonstration
promotional video
reception
suite

Communication
cell phone
correspondence
courier
interoffice mail
memo
pager
voice mail

Verbs

delete
interrupt
postpone
put off
staff
work out (a schedule)

Expressions

No problem.
Of course.
Put that in writing.
That's a good idea.
That's the best thing to do.
That would be great.
What should we do about ___?
When you get a chance, ___.

Conversation Strategies:
Expressing Reluctance

Hmm. I'm not sure that's possible.
That might be a bit difficult.

Useful Language

Please remember to ___.
If possible, could you please ___.
May I remind you not to ___.

Modals for Requests, Offers, and Suggestions

The modal verbs **can, could, will, would, should,** and **ought to** are often used to make requests, offers, and suggestions.

- Use the **base form** of the main verb after a modal verb.

  modal   base form
  I **could schedule** the presentation for Friday.

Requests

- Use **could you**, **would you**, or **would you mind** to ask someone to do something.
- Use the base form of the verb after **could you** and **would you**.

  base form
  Could you schedule a presentation?

- Use the **-ing** form of the verb (gerund) after **would you mind**.

  gerund
  Would you mind putting that in writing?

Offers

- Use **I'll (I will)** or **should I** to offer to do something.

  I'll call him later this morning.
  Should I e-mail everyone?

Suggestions

- Use **we ought to** and **we should** to make suggestions.

  We ought to talk about the schedule.

- Use **why don't I/we** and **let's** to make suggestions.

  Why don't we put it off for the moment?
  Let's put it off for now.

Nouns

achievement
distribution channel
division
layoff
outsourcing
profit
recruiter
restructuring
stock

Business Functions

food preparation
human resources
information technology
maintenance services
real estate management
security services

Verbs

appoint
lay off
outsource
recruit
reorganize
restructure

Expressions

It sounds like a good idea.
It sounds like you're on the right track.
That's quite a change.

Conversation Strategies:
Summing Up

So, basically ____.
What I'm saying is ____.
So, overall ____.

Useful Language

We have restructured/reorganized/
   changed/started/ ____.
We are continuing to work on/improve/
   expand ____.

Present Perfect

Singular		
I		
You	have made	a profit.
He/She/It	has made	a profit.

Plural		
We		
You	have made	a profit.
They		

- Use the **present perfect** to describe something that happened at an unspecified time in the past, often when the event is important in the present.

  *The company **has appointed** a new CEO recently.*

  *Sales **have fallen** sharply.*

Simple Past

- Use the **simple past** to describe something that happened at a specific time in the past.

  *Comco **appointed** a new CEO last week.*

  *Sales **fell** sharply last month.*

Nouns

data
deadline
inventory
invoice
progress report
strike
technician

Customer Service
complaint form
feedback
inconvenience
technical support

Expressions

I'd appreciate it.
I'm sorry for the delay.
I'm sorry you've been waiting so long.
It's really taking too long.
Would that help?
Would that work for you?

Wh- questions

How can I help you?
What can I do for you?

Conversation Strategies: Ending a Conversation by Promising Action

OK. I'll tell you what. I'll _____.
Anyway, why don't I _____?
All right. Let me discuss this with _____,
    and I'll get back to you.

Useful Language

Please accept our apologies for any
    inconvenience.
I've checked your account carefully
    and ___.
Unfortunately, due to ___.

Quantity Expressions

With Count (Plural) Nouns	With Non-count Nouns
a lot of	a lot of
too **many**	too **much**
as **many** as possible	as **much** as possible
not enough	not enough
not **many**	not **much**
a **few**	a **little**

Too . . ./too much/many . . .
- Use *too* before *much/many* and before
  an adjective or adverb.

  There's **too much** work.

  adjective
  Our inventory is **too low**.

  adverb
  It's taking **too long**.

Enough
- Use *enough* before a noun but after an
  adjective or adverb.

  noun
  There aren't **enough** goods in stock.

  adjective
  The service isn't good **enough**.

SUMMARY LANGUAGE

UNIT 10

Nouns

client base
joint venture
location
range (of services)

Telecommunications

charges
rates
service plan
service provider

Presentations

equipment
handout
projector
visuals

Adjectives

corporate
cutting-edge
overseas
residential

Verbs

excel
maintain
maximize

Expressions

by word of mouth
I wouldn't rule that out.
It's in the cards.
We'll go public.

Conversation Strategies:

Asking for an Opinion

What do you think about ___?
Would you agree that we should ___?
Do you think it's a good idea to ___?

Useful Language

To achieve our goals, we will ___.
To compete effectively, we will ___.

Future Forms

Aim to/plan to/be going to

- Use **aim to, plan to,** and **be going to** to talk about future plans.

  We **aim to** reach our sales target of $50 million for the year.

  We **plan to** expand our operations in Latin America next year.

  We**'re going to** introduce a new service plan.

Expect to/should/will probably

- Use **expect to, should,** and **will probably** to talk about something that could happen in the future.

  We **expect to** reduce phone charges.

  We **should** maintain our strong financial position into the next decade.

  The company **will probably** become a public company.

Might/be thinking of

- Use **might** and **be thinking of** to talk about something that is just a possibility.

  We **might** consider joint ventures with overseas Internet companies.

  We**'re thinking of** lowering international rates.

Nouns

demand
discount
feature
warranty

Technology
battery
DVD player
floppy disk
megabyte (MB)
memory
modem
RAM (Random Access Memory)
speaker
weight
zoom lens

Adjectives

aggressive	standard
compact	stylish
external	tiny
honest	wireless
slim	

Verbs

input   persuade

Expressions

Is it competitively priced?
It's a better product.
It uses the latest technology.
Our customers are always looking for ___.
There's a lot of demand for ___.

Wh- questions

How does it compare price-wise?
How does it compare to ___?
How is it different from ___?

Conversation Strategies:
Correcting Information

Actually, it's not fifty-three. It's sixty-three.
Sorry. I meant to say three hours, not six.
No, there is an internal modem.

Useful Language

In response to customer demand, we are
    introducing _____.
Please emphasize these features to our
    customers/clients/sales force.

Measurements

megabyte (MB)
ounce (oz)
pound (lb)
inch (in)
centimeter (cm)
kilogram (kg)

- With measurements, nouns following
  numbers are usually singular.

  *It has a fourteen-**inch** screen.*

Superlative Forms

It's	**the smallest** camera on the market.	
It uses	**the latest** technology.	
It's	**the most powerful** on the market.	
It has	**the most** features.	
Our	**biggest** flat-panel computer monitor is selling well.	

Comparative Forms

It's	**lighter**	
It's	**heavier**	} **than** the Portacall.
It's	**more expensive**	
It has	**more features**	

The battery lasts **longer** **than** the Portacall's.

Nouns

absenteeism	policy
choice	priority
deadline	project
globalization	risk taker
guideline	status
leader	talent
option	team player

Benefits

benefits package	health insurance
bonus	pension plan
credit card	perk
flextime	vacation
health club membership	

Adjectives

adaptable	loyal
cautious	necessary
creative	sensitive
desirable	short-staffed

Verbs

attract	reassign	recruit

Expressions

I guess you're right.
I see your point.
on short notice
That's easier said than done.
There's no other option.

Wh- questions

How's the project going?
What's the status of ___?

Conversation Strategies:
Asking for an Explanation

Why do you say that?
Could you explain that?
I don't quite see what you mean.

Useful Language

Everybody agreed that we need ___.
There was considerable discussion
   about ___.
He pointed out that ___.
She agreed/offered to ___.

Modals of Obligations and Possibility

Have to

- Use **have to/has to** to describe obligation.

  *David **has to** have your sales figures by the end of the day.*

- The past form of **have to** is **had to**.

  *I **had to** change my flight.*

- The future form of **have to** is **will/won't have to**.

  *We**'ll have to** get some more people.*

Can

- Use **can** and **can't** to describe ability and possibility.

  *If you **can't** do it, maybe Maria will help.*

- Use **was/were/will be able to** for a specific event in the past or the future.

  *We **won't be able to** meet the deadline.*

Otherwise

- **Otherwise** means "if not."

  *We don't have a choice. We won't be able to meet the deadline **otherwise** (if we don't).*

Nouns

agenda
budget
estimate
flip chart
motivation
objective
opportunity
participant
productivity
quota
turnover
white-collar worker

Adjectives

effective
productive

Verbs

brainstorm
keep up with
participate

Expressions

Absolutely.
Frankly___.
How do you feel about that?
I realize that.
If you ask me, ___.
In my opinion ___.
That's a good point.
To be honest___.
We'll be in real trouble.

Conversation Strategies:
Agreeing with Reservations

I see what you mean. But if we do
    that, ___.
That's a good point. But it doesn't solve the
    problem of ___.
I agree. But we also need to consider ___.

Useful Language

present results/estimates
review ____ plans
brainstorm possible solutions
make a decision

Real Conditions with *if . . . will*

- Use an *if* **clause** and the **future** *(will)* to talk about something that will happen under certain conditions. The *if* clause states the condition. The result clause states the probable result.

    if clause
    If *employees participate in decisions,*

    result clause
    they **will** *feel more responsible.*

- Use the **simple present** in the *if* clause and the **future** in the result clause.

    present
    If workers **get** *performance bonuses,*

    future
    they **will be** *more productive.*

SUMMARY LANGUAGE

UNIT 14

Nouns

carton
facilities
flavor
laundry detergent
link
soft drink
superstition

Advertising

advertising campaign
audience
billboard
cartoon character
consumer
home page
TV air time
TV commercial

Verbs

advertise
aim at
appeal to
place
reach

Adjectives

appropriate
attractive
luxurious

Expressions

Any ideas?
Any suggestions?
If I were you, I'd ___.
It would be nice if we could ___.
Maybe we could go for both.

Conversation Strategies:
Moving a Discussion Forward

We need to move on.
We don't have much time left.
   Let's discuss ___.
OK. Are we ready to decide?

Useful Language

I would not recommend ___.
___ would be more suitable for our market.
I would suggest ___.

Unreal Conditions with *Would* and *Could*

• Use an *if* clause and **would** or **could** to talk about something that is contrary to fact, that is not the real situation, or that is a possibility.

If I were you, I **would** *look at websites for teenagers.*

• When the verb in a sentence is **would** or **could** plus the base form, the verb in the *if* clause is often in the past tense.

                  past
Billboards **could** *work if we* **focused** *on subway advertising.*

What if . . .

• Use **what if** and **past tense** to suggest a possibility.

          past
What if *we* **advertised** *on billboards?*

GLOSSARY

ADVERTISE (v) 1. to tell people about a product, event, or service in order to persuade them to buy or use it. 2. to make an announcement in a newspaper asking for someone to work for you.

ADVERTISING CAMPAIGN a connected set of actions intended to encourage people to buy a product or a service.

AGENDA a list of the subjects to be discussed at a meeting.

APPOINT (v) to choose someone for a job, position, etc.

BENEFIT something a company gives its employees in addition to salary, such as health insurance or a pension plan.

BENEFITS PACKAGE all the benefits that a company offers its employees.

BONUS money given to an employee in addition to pay or salary.

BRAINSTORM (v) to meet with someone or a group in order to try to develop ideas and think of ways to solve problems.

BUDGET a plan of how to spend the money that is available in a particular period of time, or the money itself.

BUSINESS TO BUSINESS the selling of goods and services from one company to another.

CANDIDATE someone who applies or is being considered for a job or position.

COMMUTE (v) to travel regularly in order to get to work.

CONSUMER someone who buys or uses goods and services.

CORPORATION an organization or company that is owned by shareholders.

CUSTOMER someone who buys goods or services from a company, store, etc.

CUSTOMER SERVICE the department of a company that helps its clients or customers and also deals with problems or complaints.

DATA information, facts, and numbers.

DEADLINE a time by which someone must finish a project or task.

DISCOUNT a reduction in the usual price of something.

DISTRIBUTION the process of getting goods to consumers.

DISTRIBUTION CENTER the place where goods are stored, sorted, and shipped to stores or customers.

DIVISION a group or department within a company or organization.

DRESS CODE rules about the type of clothes employees should wear at a particular company.

EARNINGS PER SHARE income to stockholders for each share owned.

E-COMMERCE the buying and selling of goods and services over the Internet.

E-MAIL (ELECTRONIC MAIL) a system in which you can send letters from your computer or PDA to another computer or PDA.

EVALUATE (v) to carefully consider something or someone in order to judge him, her, or it.

EXECUTIVE someone whose job it is to decide what a company or business will do.

FACILITIES rooms, equipment, or services that are provided for a particular purpose.

FAST TRACK a career path with quick promotion for talented employees.

FAX a document that is sent in electronic form down a telephone line and then printed using a special machine.

FINANCE   the management of money, especially for a company.

FLEXTIME   a system in which employees can change the times at which they start and finish the work day.

GOAL   something that a person or a company wants to achieve in the future.

GOODS   things that are produced in order to be sold.

HEAD OFFICE   the main office of a company. Also called the company "headquarters."

HOMEPAGE   (n) the first or main page of a website for a company, a person, or an organization.

HUMAN RESOURCES   the department of a company that deals with hiring and training employees.

INCOME   money that is earned from work, sales, or investments.

INTEROFFICE MAIL   memos or communications from one part of a company to another.

INVENTORY   all the goods that a company or store has available for sale.

INVOICE   a list that shows how much is owed for goods or services.

JOB   work that a person does regularly in order to earn money.

JOINT VENTURE   a business arrangement in which two or more companies work together to achieve something.

LAPTOP (COMPUTER)   a small computer that a person can carry.

LAY OFF   (phrasal v) to stop employing someone, especially when there is not enough work to do.

LINK   a reference to another page or a website on the Internet.

LOGO   a small design that is the official sign of a company or organization.

MANAGEMENT   the people who are in charge of a company or organization.

MANAGER   someone who directs the work of a business or organization.

MANUFACTURE   (n) the process of making goods, usually in large numbers. (v) to use machines to make goods, usually in large numbers.

MARKET   the geographical area or a group of people that a company sells products or services to.

MARKET SHARE   the percentage of the market for a product or service that a company supplies.

MODEM   a device that allows a computer to communicate with another computer over a standard telephone line.

MOTIVATION   1. eagerness and willingness to do something. 2. the reason why a person wants to do something.

NET INCOME   the amount of income a business or a person receives when nothing further is to be subtracted (after taxes and other expenses are paid).

OUTSOURCING   the practice of hiring an outside company or person to handle a part of a company's internal operations.

OVERTIME   time that an employee works in addition to the usual working hours.

PAGER   a small machine that fits in a pocket and makes a sound when someone is telephoning; beeper.

PARTNERSHIP   a business owned and operated by two or more people.

PDA (PERSONAL DIGITAL ASSISTANT)   a hand-held computerized organizer for addresses, appointments, and e-mail.

PERFORMANCE BONUS money given to an employee (in addition to salary) for good work.

PERK (PERQUISITE) money, goods, or other advantages that an employee gets from a job in addition to pay.

PLANT a factory and all its equipment.

POLICY a way of doing things that has been officially agreed on and chosen by a company or organization.

PRESENTATION a formal talk about a particular subject or product.

PRESENTER a person who gives a speech or talk at a meeting.

PRODUCTIVE (adj.) producing or achieving a lot.

PRODUCTIVITY the rate at which goods are produced.

PROFIT money that a business or a person gains by selling products or services.

PROMOTION advancement to a higher position at a job.

QUALITY CONTROL the practice of checking goods as they are produced to make sure that they are well made.

QUOTA 1. a particular amount that someone is expected to have. 2. a limit on the amount of something a person is allowed to have.

RAM (RANDOM ACCESS MEMORY) the part of a computer that keeps information for a short time so that it can be used immediately.

RECRUIT (v) to find new people to work in a company, join an organization, do a job, etc.

REP (REPRESENTATIVE) someone in a company who sells products or services.

RESTRUCTURE (v) to change the way in which something such as a business or system is organized.

RETAILER someone who sells goods to the public through a store, the mail, or on the Internet.

SALARY money that an employee is given for working; pay.

SALESPERSON someone whose job it is to sell goods or services.

SCHEDULE a plan of what someone is going to do and the time it will take to do it.

SENIORITY the state of being higher in rank than someone else in a company or organization.

SERVICE (v) to provide people with something that they need.

SHIP (v) 1. to deliver goods. 2. to send or carry something by land, sea, or air.

SHIPMENT a load of goods being delivered, or the act of sending them.

SHORT-STAFFED (adj.) having too few employees.

SMALL TALK polite, friendly, social conversation.

STAFF (n) the people who work for a company or a department of a company. (v) to provide workers for an organization.

STOCK 1. a supply of something that is kept to be sold or used later. 2. a share in a company. 3. the number of shares that a person owns, or the total value of a company's shares.

STRATEGY the set of plans and skills used in order to gain success or achieve a goal.

SUPPLIER a company that provides a particular product.

SUPPLY (v) to provide people with something that they need or want, especially regularly over a long time.

TEAM a group of people who to work together on a particular project or task.

TEAMWORK the ability of a group to work well together, or the effort the group makes.

TECHNICAL SUPPORT 1. the people or department of a company that helps maintain computers, software, printers, etc. 2. the people in a computer or software company who help customers with problems they may have with equipment or programs.

TELECOMMUNICATIONS the business of sending and receiving messages by radio, telephone, satellite, etc.

TRADE SHOW an exhibit where the same types of companies show their products.

TRAINING the process of teaching or being taught skills needed for a particular job.

UPDATE the most recent news about something.

VICE PRESIDENT 1. a person who is next in rank to the president of company. 2. someone who is responsible for a particular part of a company.

VIDEOCONFERENCE a meeting where people who cannot attend in person can participate via a video monitor.

VISUAL (VISUAL AID) a graph, chart, or picture that is used to help people to understand something.

VOICEMAIL a system, especially in a company, in which telephone messages are recorded so that someone can listen to them later.

WAREHOUSE a large building for storing quantities of goods.

WEBSITE a place on the Internet that and gives information about a particular company, subject, or product.

WORLDWIDE (adj.) everywhere in the world, or within the whole world.

N = north
E = east
S = south
W = west

Hanjin Shipping	*www.hanjin.com*		**Pepsi**	*www.pepsi.com*
Hewlett Packard	*www.hp.com*		**Plantronics**	*www.plantronics.com*
Honda	*www.honda.com*		**Swatch**	*www.swatch.com*
IBM	*www.ibm.com*		**Tropicana**	*www.tropicana.com*
Intuit	*www.intuit.com*		**Varig**	*www.varig.com*
Kodak	*www.kodak.com*		**Unibanco**	*www.unibanco.com.br*
Lucent Technologies	*www.lucent.com*		**UPS**	*www.ups.com*
NTT Communications	*www.ntt.com*			

The publisher would like to thank the following for permission to reproduce logos:

pages 5 and 86: Pepsico Corporation; International Business Machines Corporation; Eastman Kodak Company; Lucent Technologies.

page 32: Tropicana Products, Inc.

GLOBAL LINKS 2.

English for International Business

Phrase Book

Angela Blackwell

Longman

Unit 1 Talking About Your Company

Nouns

annual income
client
corporation
dress code
employee

executive
head office
headset
suit
supplier

Industries

banking
consulting services
finance/financial services
Internet services

shipping
telecommunications
transportation

Adjectives and Adverbs

casual (adj.)
formal/informal (adj.)
worldwide (adv.)

Verbs

design
develop
employ
expand
hire

manufacture
market
provide
sell
supply

Expressions

Are you based in ___?
Oh.
Really?
That's interesting.
What does your company do?

Conversation Strategies:

Clarifying Information

Could you repeat that?
Excuse me?
How do you spell that?

Useful Language

We are recognized as a world leader in _____.
Enclosed is a catalogue that describes _____.
Please feel free to call me for further information.

Simple Present

Affirmative Statements

I	**work**	We	
You	**work**	You }	**work**
He/She/It	**works**	They	

Negative Statements

I	**don't** }	
He/She/It	**doesn't**	**work**

We }		
You	**don't**	**work**
They		

Present Continuous

Affirmative and Negative Statements

I	**am** }	
You	**are**	(not) **working**
He/She/It	**is**	

We }	**are**	(not) **working**
They		

- Use the **simple present** to describe something that is always true or true in general.

  *Plantronics Inc. **designs** and **manufactures** lightweight headsets.*

- Use the **present continuous** to describe something that is true at the moment or for a limited time.

  *Plantronics is currently **marketing** its products for home use.*

Nouns

paperwork
software engineer
training

Socializing

bill	meal
business lunch	menu
city	mineral water
coffee	small talk
fan (sports)	soccer
food	sports
guest	tea
host	trip

Adjectives

delicious	nice
excellent	popular
exciting	wonderful

Verbs

enjoy   order   like

Expressions

Actually . . .
Can I get you something to drink?
Could I get you a cup of coffee?
Did you have a good trip?
How's it going?
No, thanks.
Right.
That's right.
Would you like some help with the menu?

Wh- questions

What do you recommend?
What do you think of ___?
What part of ___ are you from?
What would you like to drink?

Conversation Strategies:

Making Small Talk

You're from ___, aren't you?
Is this your first visit to ___?
Do you like ___?
You enjoy ___, don't you?
Tell me, do you follow ___? (a sport)
What about you?

Useful Language

I appreciated your feedback about ___.
As I mentioned during lunch, ___.

Tag Questions

A **tag question** is a question added at the end of a sentence.
If the statement is affirmative, the tag is usually negative.
If the statement is negative, the tag is usually affirmative.

Affirmative Statement + Negative Tag

---

*It's a wonderful city, **isn't it**?*
*That **was** a wonderful meal, **wasn't it**?*
*You live in Sao Paulo, **don't you**?*

Negative Statement + Affirmative Tag

---

*You **aren't** in the computer industry, **are you**?*
*You **don't** follow soccer much, **do you**?*

- Use a tag question to check that something is true.

  *You're in the computer industry, **aren't you**?*

- Use a tag question when you think the other person will agree.

  *It's a wonderful city, **isn't it**?*

Nouns

calendar
commute
gesture
manufacturing plant
rush hour
schedule
sightseeing
system
videoconferencing

Events

meeting (planning, sales)
presentation (design, sales)
appointment
flight
trade show

Verbs

arrange
arrive
schedule

Expressions

Are you available the next day?
Could we set up a meeting?
How about the 25th?
. . . if it's convenient for you.
. . . if it's OK with you.
I'm afraid I can't make it.
I'm sorry, I'm busy on ___.
I'm free after ___.
That sounds good.
That's OK with me.
When can you make it?

Conversation Strategies:

Accepting an Invitation

I'd like to (have dinner).
That would be very nice. Thank you.
That would be great.

Useful Language

If possible, I would like to ___.
Could you please suggest ___?
I'm afraid I won't be available ___.

The Simple Present and Present Continuous for the Future

- Use the **simple present** for scheduled future events. Use the **present continuous** to refer to future plans.

Simple Present for the Future

The plane **leaves** at noon.

Present Continuous for the Future

I'm **coming** to Sydney next month.

Prepositions of Time: *At, In, On*

- Use **at** with time expressions.
  at *nine o'clock*, **at** *ten-fifteen*, **at** *noon*
- Use **in** with *the morning, the afternoon, the evening.*
  in *the morning*
- Use **on** with a day or a date.
  on *Monday*, **on** *the 20th*, **on** *my birthday*

Nouns

candidate
colleague
computer skills
degree
experience
fast track
management

marketing
position
product development
promotion
recommendation
research and
   development (R&D)

Job Titles

accountant
assistant (executive, administrative)
CEO (Chief Executive Officer)
chairwoman
director
president
sales representative (rep)
vice president

Adjectives

current   senior   previous

Verbs

graduate   recommend   promote

Expressions

I'm delighted to hear that.
I'm with (name of company).
I've wanted to meet you for a long time.
That's excellent news.
What area are you in?

Conversation Strategies:
Disagreeing Politely

I'm not sure I agree.
Do you think so?
Yes, but don't you think ___?

Useful Language

He/She has been with the company for ___ years.

He/She first worked in ___.

He/She took over as ___.

For the past ___ years, he/she has worked in ___.

Present Perfect Tense

Regular verbs and the verb *be*

Singular		
I You }	**have** (not) {	worked been
He/She/It	**has** (not) {	worked been

Plural		
We You They }	**have** (not) {	worked been

- Use the **present perfect** to talk about actions and situations that began in the past and continue in the present.

  Fiorina **has been** at Hewlett-Packard since 1997.

Prepositions of Time: *For* and *Since*; *How long . . .?*

- Use **for** to describe a period of time.

  Fiorina has held senior management positions **for** 20 years.

- Use **since** to describe a point in time.

  She has been at Hewlett-Packard **since** 1997.

- **How long** is often used with the present perfect.

  How long have you been in this position?

UNIT 5 TURING A COMPANY AROUND

Nouns

competition
competitor
customer satisfaction
goal
image
keyboard
laptop
logo
market

market share
model
morale
peak
route
sales
sales performance
strategy
survey

Adjectives

falling
flat

increasing
(un)profitable

Adverbs

dramatically
immediately

steadily

Verbs

invest
redesign

reduce
understand

Verbs to Describe Performance

fall
improve
increase
rise

drop
reach (a peak)
remain (flat)

Expressions

Did you figure it out?
It didn't perform well.
So, what did you do?
We couldn't understand it.

Past Time Expressions

a few years ago
in the early/mid/late 90's
last year

Conversation Strategies:
Controlling the Flow of Information

Just a minute.
Can we back up a minute?
Let me get that down.

Useful Language

We required flight attendants to ___.
We installed/redesigned ___.
We assigned more personnel to ___.
As a result, ___.

Simple Past
Affirmative Statements

Regular Verbs	
save	They **save**d the industry.
launch	They **launch**ed the Swatch brand.

Irregular Verbs	
be	The strategy **was** a success.
fall	Sales **fell** in 1983.
go	A sales team **went** to America.

Negative Statements	
be	The strategy **wasn't** a success.
fall	Sales **didn't fall** in 2000.
go	A sales team **didn't go** to America.

Questions	
be	**Was** it a success?
do	What **did** you **do**?

Past Forms of Other Irregular Verbs

find	**found**	make	**made**
have	**had**	rise	**rose**
know	**knew**	sell	**sold**
lose	**lost**		

Nouns

e-commerce
delivery process
hiring process
online
performance
position
process

production
résumé
status
system
team
training
Web

Shipping and Delivery

cart
conveyor belt
delivery
distribution center
package

shelf
shipment
supplier
warehouse

Adjectives

interesting   two-step   top

Verbs

advertise
deliver
evaluate
interview
place
rank
remove

review
select
ship
sort
store
unload

Sequencers

First . . .   After that . . .   Finally . . .
Then . . .   Next . . .

Expressions

Here's how it works.
How does your management training system work?
How's that done?
I see.
Let me explain.
That's an interesting system/process.

Conversation Strategies:

Checking for Understanding

Do you want me to repeat that?
Do you have any questions?
Is that clear?

Useful Language

The items are back ordered/out of stock/ready for shipment.
The order was shipped this morning/incorrectly
addressed/refused by customs.

The Passive Voice: Simple Present and Simple Past

Simple Present

The fruit	**is washed.**	
The employees	**are ranked.**	
The evaluations	**are done**	every year.
The packages	**are put**	on a truck.

Simple Past

The order	**was shipped**	last Tuesday.
The items	**were delivered**	this morning.
The box	**was taken**	off the shelf.

- Use the **passive voice** to describe processes and procedures
  when the focus is on the action that is done rather than on
  the person who does the action.

Nouns

Trade Fairs and Conventions

accommodation
booth
brochure
conference center
product demonstration
promotional video
reception
suite

Communication

cell phone
correspondence
courier
interoffice mail
memo
pager
voice mail

Verbs

delete
interrupt
postpone
put off
staff
work out (a schedule)

Expressions

No problem.
Of course.
Put that in writing.
That's a good idea.
That's the best thing to do.
That would be great.
What should we do about ___?
When you get a chance, ___.

Conversation Strategies:

Expressing Reluctance

Hmm. I'm not sure that's possible.
That might be a bit difficult.

Useful Language

Please remember to ___.
If possible, could you please ___.
May I remind you not to ___.

Modals for Requests, Offers, and Suggestions

The modal verbs *can*, *could*, *will*, *would*, *should*, and *ought to* are often used to make requests, offers, and suggestions.

- Use the **base form** of the main verb after a modal verb.

  <small>modal   base form</small>
  I **could schedule** the presentation for Friday.

Requests

- Use *could you*, *would you*, or *would you mind* to ask someone to do something.
- Use the base form of the verb after *could you* and *would you*.

  <small>base form</small>
  Could you schedule a presentation?

- Use the *-ing* form of the verb (gerund) after *would you mind*.

  <small>gerund</small>
  Would you mind putting that in writing?

Offers

- Use *I'll (I will)* or *should I* to offer to do something.

  I'll call him later this morning.
  Should I e-mail everyone?

Suggestions

- Use *we ought to* and *we should* to make suggestions.

  We ought to talk about the schedule.

- Use *why don't I/we* and *let's* to make suggestions.

  Why don't we put it off for the moment?
  Let's put it off for now.

Nouns

achievement
distribution channel
division
layoff
outsourcing
profit
recruiter
restructuring
stock

Business Functions

food preparation
human resources
information technology
maintenance services
real estate management
security services

Verbs

appoint
lay off
outsource
recruit
reorganize
restructure

Expressions

It sounds like a good idea.
It sounds like you're on the right track.
That's quite a change.

Conversation Strategies:
Summing Up

So, basically ____.
What I'm saying is ____.
So, overall ____.

Useful Language

We have restructured/reorganized/
changed/started/ ____.
We are continuing to work on/improve/ expand ____.

Present Perfect

Singular		
I You	**have made**	a profit.
He/She/It	**has made**	a profit.

Plural		
We You They	**have made**	a profit.

- Use the **present perfect** to describe something that happened at an unspecified time in the past, often when the event is important in the present.

  *The company **has appointed** a new CEO recently.*

  *Sales **have fallen** sharply.*

Simple Past

- Use the **simple past** to describe something that happened at a specific time in the past.

  *Comco **appointed** a new CEO last week.*

  *Sales **fell** sharply last month.*

Nouns

data
deadline
inventory
invoice
progress report
strike
technician

Customer Service

complaint form
feedback
inconvenience
technical support

Expressions

I'd appreciate it.
I'm sorry for the delay.
I'm sorry you've been waiting so long.
It's really taking too long.
Would that help?
Would that work for you?

Wh- questions

How can I help you?
What can I do for you?

Conversation Strategies:

Ending a Conversation by Promising Action

OK. I'll tell you what. I'll _____.
Anyway, why don't I _____?
All right. Let me discuss this with _____, and I'll
    get back to you.

Useful Language

Please accept our apologies for any inconvenience.

I've checked your account carefully and ___.

Unfortunately, due to ___.

Quantity Expressions

With Count (Plural) Nouns	With Non-count Nouns
a lot of	a lot of
too **many**	too **much**
as **many** as possible	as **much** as possible
not enough	not enough
not **many**	not **much**
a **few**	a **little**

Too . . ./too much/many . . .

- Use *too* before *much/many* and before an adjective or adverb.

  There's *too much* work.

  Our inventory is *too low*.

  adjective

  It's taking *too long*.

  adverb

Enough

- Use enough before a noun but after an adjective or adverb.

  There aren't **enough** goods in stock.

  noun

  The service isn't good **enough**.

  adjective

UNIT 10 CORPORATE GOALS

Nouns

client base
joint venture
location
range (of services)

Telecommunications

charges
rates
service plan
service provider

Presentations

equipment
handout
projector
visuals

Adjectives

corporate
cutting-edge
overseas
residential

Verbs

excel
maintain
maximize

Expressions

by word of mouth
I wouldn't rule that out.
It's in the cards.
We'll go public.

Conversation Strategies:

Asking for an Opinion

What do you think about ___?
Would you agree that we should ___?
Do you think it's a good idea to ___?

Useful Language

To achieve our goals, we will ___.
To compete effectively, we will ___.

Future Forms

Aim to/plan to/be going to

- Use **aim to**, **plan to**, and **be going to**
  to talk about future plans.

  We **aim to** reach our sales target of $50
  million for the year.

  We **plan to** expand our operations in
  Latin America next year.

  We**'re going to** introduce a new service
  plan.

Expect to/should/will probably

- Use **expect to**, **should**, and **will probably**
  to talk about something that could
  happen in the future.

  We **expect to** reduce phone charges.

  We **should** maintain our strong financial
  position into the next decade.

  The company **will probably** become a
  public company.

Might/be thinking of

- Use **might** and **be thinking of** to talk
  about something that is just a possibility.

  We **might** consider joint ventures with
  overseas Internet companies.

  We**'re thinking of** lowering international
  rates.

UNIT 11 DESCRIBING AND COMPARING PRODUCTS

Nouns

demand
discount
feature
warranty

Technology

battery
DVD player
floppy disk
megabyte (MB)
memory
modem
RAM (Random Access Memory)
speaker
weight
zoom lens

Adjectives

aggressive	standard
compact	stylish
external	tiny
honest	wireless
slim	

Verbs

input	persuade

Expressions

Is it competitively priced?
It's a better product.
It uses the latest technology.
Our customers are always looking for ___.
There's a lot of demand for ___.

Wh- questions

How does it compare price-wise?
How does it compare to ___?
How is it different from ___?

Conversation Strategies:

Correcting Information

Actually, it's not fifty-three. It's sixty-three.

Sorry. I meant to say three hours, not six.

No, there is an internal modem.

Useful Language

In response to customer demand, we are introducing _____.

Please emphasize these features to our
    customers/clients/sales force.

Measurements

megabyte (MB)

ounce (oz)

pound (lb)

inch (in)

centimeter (cm)

kilogram (kg)

- With measurements, nouns following
  numbers are usually singular.

  *It has a fourteen-**inch** screen.*

Superlative Forms

It's	**the smallest** camera on the market.
It uses	**the latest** technology.
It's	**the most powerful** on the market.
It has	**the most** features.
Our	**biggest** flat-panel computer monitor is selling well.

Comparative Forms

It's	**lighter**	
It's	**heavier**	**than** the Portacall.
It's	**more expensive**	
It has	**more features**	

The battery lasts **longer**   **than** the Portacall's.

Nouns

absenteeism	policy
choice	priority
deadline	project
globalization	risk taker
guideline	status
leader	talent
option	team player

Benefits

benefits package	health insurance
bonus	pension plan
credit card	perk
flextime	vacation
health club membership	

Adjectives

adaptable	loyal
cautious	necessary
creative	sensitive
desirable	short-staffed

Verbs

attract	reassign	recruit

Expressions

I guess you're right.
I see your point.
on short notice
That's easier said than done.
There's no other option.

Wh- questions

How's the project going?
What's the status of ___?

Conversation Strategies:

Asking for an Explanation

Why do you say that?
Could you explain that?
I don't quite see what you mean.

Useful Language

Everybody agreed that we need ___.
There was considerable discussion about ___.
He pointed out that ___.
She agreed/offered to ___.

Modals of Obligations and Possibility

Have to

- Use **have to/has to** to describe obligation.

  David **has to** have your sales figures by the end of the day.

- The past form of **have to** is **had to**.

  I **had to** change my flight.

- The future form of **have to** is **will/won't have to**.

  We'll **have to** get some more people.

Can

- Use **can** and **can't** to describe ability and possibility.

  If you **can't** do it, maybe Maria will help.

- Use **was/were/will be able to** for a specific event in the past or the future.

  We **won't be able to** meet the deadline.

Otherwise

- **Otherwise** means "if not."

  We don't have a choice. We won't be able to meet the deadline **otherwise** (if we don't).

Nouns

agenda
budget
estimate
flip chart
motivation
objective
opportunity
participant
productivity
quota
turnover
white-collar worker

Adjectives

effective
productive

Verbs

brainstorm
keep up with
participate

Expressions

Absolutely.
Frankly___.
How do you feel about that?
I realize that.
If you ask me, ___.
In my opinion ___.
That's a good point.
To be honest___.
We'll be in real trouble.

Conversation Strategies:

Agreeing with Reservations

I see what you mean. But if we do that, ___.
That's a good point. But it doesn't solve the problem of ___.
I agree. But we also need to consider ___.

Useful Language

present results/estimates
review ___ plans
brainstorm possible solutions
make a decision

Real Conditions with *if . . . will*

- Use an *if* **clause** and the **future** *(will)* to talk about
  something that will happen under certain conditions.
  The *if* clause states the condition. The result clause
  states the probable result.

  if clause
  If employees participate in decisions,

  result clause
  they **will** feel more responsible.

- Use the **simple present** in the *if* clause and the **future**
  in the result clause.

  present
  If workers **get** performance bonuses,

  future
  they **will be** more productive.

Nouns

carton
facilities
flavor
laundry detergent
link
soft drink
superstition

Advertising

advertising campaign
audience
billboard
cartoon character
consumer
home page
TV air time
TV commercial

Verbs

advertise
aim at
appeal to
place
reach

Adjectives

appropriate
attractive
luxurious

Expressions

Any ideas?
Any suggestions?
If I were you, I'd ___.
It would be nice if we could ___.
Maybe we could go for both.

Conversation Strategies:

Moving a Discussion Forward

We need to move on.
We don't have much time left.
    Let's discuss ___.
OK. Are we ready to decide?

Useful Language

I would not recommend ___.
___ would be more suitable for our market.
I would suggest ___.

Unreal Conditions with Would and Could

- Use an *if* clause and **would** or **could** to talk about something
  that is contrary to fact, that is not the real situation, or that
  is a possibility.

  *If I were you, I **would** look at websites for teenagers.*

- When the verb in a sentence is **would** or **could** plus the
  base form, the verb in the *if* clause is often in the past tense.

  *Billboards **could** work if we **focused** on subway advertising.*

  (*focused* — past)

What if . . .

- Use **what if** and **past tense** to suggest a possibility.

  ***What if we advertised** on billboards?*

  (*advertised* — past)

ADVERTISE (v) 1. to tell people about a product, event, or service in order to persuade them to buy or use it. 2. to make an announcement in a newspaper asking for someone to work for you.

ADVERTISING CAMPAIGN a connected set of actions intended to encourage people to buy a product or a service.

AGENDA a list of the subjects to be discussed at a meeting.

APPOINT (v) to choose someone for a job, position, etc.

BENEFIT something a company gives its employees in addition to salary, such as health insurance or a pension plan.

BENEFITS PACKAGE all the benefits that a company offers its employees.

BONUS money given to an employee in addition to pay or salary.

BRAINSTORM (v) to meet with someone or a group in order to try to develop ideas and think of ways to solve problems.

BUDGET a plan of how to spend the money that is available in a particular period of time, or the money itself.

BUSINESS TO BUSINESS the selling of goods and services from one company to another.

CANDIDATE someone who applies or is being considered for a job or position.

COMMUTE (v) to travel regularly in order to get to work.

CONSUMER someone who buys or uses goods and services.

CORPORATION an organization or company that is owned by shareholders.

CUSTOMER someone who buys goods or services from a company, store, etc.

CUSTOMER SERVICE the department of a company that helps its clients or customers and also deals with problems or complaints.

DATA information, facts, and numbers.

DEADLINE a time by which someone must finish a project or task.

DISCOUNT a reduction in the usual price of something.

DISTRIBUTION the process of getting goods to consumers.

DISTRIBUTION CENTER the place where goods are stored, sorted, and shipped to stores or customers.

DIVISION a group or department within a company or organization.

DRESS CODE rules about the type of clothes employees should wear at a particular company.

EARNINGS PER SHARE income to stockholders for each share owned.

E-COMMERCE the buying and selling of goods and services over the Internet.

E-MAIL (ELECTRONIC MAIL) a system in which you can send letters from your computer or PDA to another computer or PDA.

EVALUATE (v) to carefully consider something or someone in order to judge him, her, or it.

EXECUTIVE someone whose job it is to decide what a company or business will do.

FACILITIES rooms, equipment, or services that are provided for a particular purpose.

FAST TRACK a career path with quick promotion for talented employees.

FAX a document that is sent in electronic form down a telephone line and then printed using a special machine.

FINANCE the management of money, especially for a company.

FLEXTIME a system in which employees can change the times at which they start and finish the work day.

GOAL something that a person or a company wants to achieve in the future.

GOODS things that are produced in order to be sold.

HEAD OFFICE the main office of a company. Also called the company "headquarters."

HOMEPAGE (n) the first or main page of a website for a company, a person, or an organization.

HUMAN RESOURCES the department of a company that deals with hiring and training employees.

INCOME money that is earned from work, sales, or investments.

INTEROFFICE MAIL memos or communications from one part of a company to another.

INVENTORY all the goods that a company or store has available for sale.

INVOICE a list that shows how much is owed for goods or services.

JOB work that a person does regularly in order to earn money.

JOINT VENTURE a business arrangement in which two or more companies work together to achieve something.

LAPTOP (COMPUTER) a small computer that a person can carry.

LAY OFF (phrasal v) to stop employing someone, especially when there is not enough work to do.

LINK a reference to another page or a website on the Internet.

LOGO a small design that is the official sign of a company or organization.

MANAGEMENT the people who are in charge of a company or organization.

MANAGER someone who directs the work of a business or organization.

MANUFACTURE (n) the process of making goods, usually in large numbers. (v) to use machines to make goods, usually in large numbers.

MARKET the geographical area or a group of people that a company sells products or services to.

MARKET SHARE the percentage of the market for a product or service that a company supplies.

MODEM a device that allows a computer to communicate with another computer over a standard telephone line.

MOTIVATION 1. eagerness and willingness to do something. 2. the reason why a person wants to do something.

NET INCOME the amount of income a business or a person receives when nothing further is to be subtracted (after taxes and other expenses are paid).

OUTSOURCING the practice of hiring an outside company or person to handle a part of a company's internal operations.

OVERTIME time that an employee works in addition to the usual working hours.

PAGER a small machine that fits in a pocket and makes a sound when someone is telephoning; beeper.

PARTNERSHIP a business owned and operated by two or more people.

PDA (PERSONAL DIGITAL ASSISTANT) a hand-held computerized organizer for addresses, appointments, and e-mail.

PERFORMANCE BONUS money given to an employee (in addition to salary) for good work.

PERK (PERQUISITE) money, goods, or other advantages that an employee gets from a job in addition to pay.

PLANT a factory and all its equipment.

POLICY a way of doing things that has been officially agreed on and chosen by a company or organization.

PRESENTATION a formal talk about a particular subject or product.

PRESENTER a person who gives a speech or talk at a meeting.

PRODUCTIVE (adj.) producing or achieving a lot.

PRODUCTIVITY the rate at which goods are produced.

PROFIT money that a business or a person gains by selling products or services.

PROMOTION advancement to a higher position at a job.

QUALITY CONTROL the practice of checking goods as they are produced to make sure that they are well made.

QUOTA 1. a particular amount that someone is expected to have. 2. a limit on the amount of something a person is allowed to have.

RAM (RANDOM ACCESS MEMORY) the part of a computer that keeps information for a short time so that it can be used immediately.

RECRUIT (v) to find new people to work in a company, join an organization, do a job, etc.

REP (REPRESENTATIVE) someone in a company who sells products or services.

RESTRUCTURE (v) to change the way in which something such as a business or system is organized.

RETAILER someone who sells goods to the public through a store, the mail, or on the Internet.

SALARY money that an employee is given for working; pay.

SALESPERSON someone whose job it is to sell goods or services.

SCHEDULE a plan of what someone is going to do and the time it will take to do it.

SENIORITY the state of being higher in rank than someone else in a company or organization.

SERVICE (v) to provide people with something they need.

SHIP (v) 1. to deliver goods. 2. to send or carry something by land, sea, or air.

SHIPMENT a load of goods being delivered, or the act of sending them.

SHORT-STAFFED (adj.) having too few employees.

SMALL TALK polite, friendly, social conversation.

STAFF (n) the people who work for a company or a department of a company. (v) to provide workers for an organization.

STOCK 1. a supply of something that is kept to be sold or used later. 2. a share in a company. 3. the number of shares that a person owns, or the total value of a company's shares.

STRATEGY the set of plans and skills used in order to gain success or achieve a goal.

SUPPLIER a company that provides a particular product.

SUPPLY (v) to provide people with something that they need or want, especially regularly over a long time.

TEAM a group of people who to work together on a particular project or task.

TEAMWORK the ability of a group to work well together, or the effort the group makes.

TECHNICAL SUPPORT 1. the people or department of a company that helps maintain computers, software, printers, etc. 2. the people in a computer or software company who help customers with problems they may have with equipment or programs.

TELECOMMUNICATIONS the business of sending and receiving messages by radio, telephone, satellite, etc.

TRADE SHOW an exhibit where the same types of companies show their products.

TRAINING the process of teaching or being taught skills needed for a particular job.

UPDATE the most recent news about something.

VICE PRESIDENT 1. a person who is next in rank to the president of company. 2. someone who is responsible for a particular part of a company.

VIDEOCONFERENCE a meeting where people who cannot attend in person can participate via a video monitor.

VISUAL (VISUAL AID) a graph, chart, or picture that is used to help people to understand something.

VOICEMAIL a system, especially in a company, in which telephone messages are recorded so that someone can listen to them later.

WAREHOUSE a large building for storing quantities of goods.

WEBSITE a place on the Internet that and gives information about a particular company, subject, or product.

WORLDWIDE (adj.) everywhere in the world, or within the whole world.